Theodore Gilman

**A Graded Banking System Formed by the Incorporation of Clearing Houses**

Currency Secured by Pledge of Bank Assets

Theodore Gilman

**A Graded Banking System Formed by the Incorporation of Clearing Houses**
*Currency Secured by Pledge of Bank Assets*

ISBN/EAN: 9783337152253

Printed in Europe, USA, Canada, Australia, Japan

Cover: Foto ©Suzi / pixelio.de

More available books at **www.hansebooks.com**

A

# GRADED BANKING SYSTEM

FORMED BY THE INCORPORATION OF
CLEARING HOUSES UNDER
A FEDERAL LAW

WITH POWER TO ISSUE A CLEARING HOUSE
CURRENCY SECURED BY PLEDGE
OF BANK ASSETS

FOR THE PROTECTION AND SUPPORT OF COMMERCIAL
CREDIT, AND THE EQUALIZATION OF RATES
OF INTEREST THROUGHOUT
THE NATION

BY

THEODORE GILMAN

BOSTON AND NEW YORK
HOUGHTON, MIFFLIN AND COMPANY
The Riverside Press, Cambridge
1898

# CONTENTS

|  | PAGE |
|---|---|
| PREFACE | v–xvi |

### I.
THE SEPARATION OF BANKING FUNCTIONS . . . . . . 1

### II.
A COMPARISON BETWEEN GRADED AND UNGRADED OR COÖPERATIVE AND COMPETITIVE SYSTEMS . . . . . 6

### III.
THE ENGLISH SYSTEM . . . . . . . . . . . . . 14

### IV.
THE FRENCH SYSTEM . . . . . . . . . . . . . 22

### V.
THE GERMAN SYSTEM . . . . . . . . . . . . . 31

### VI.
THE UNITED STATES SYSTEM . . . . . . . . . . 38

### VII.
A DISCUSSION OF THE CONDITION OF BANKING RESERVES IN THE UNITED STATES AS THE CAUSE OF OUR FINANCIAL TROUBLES . . . . . . . . . . . . . . . . . 49

### VIII.
FALLACIOUS REMEDIES . . . . . . . . . . . . 65

## CONTENTS

### IX.

A DISCUSSION OF PRACTICAL DIFFICULTIES IN THE WAY OF A UNIVERSAL SYSTEM . . . . . . . . . . . 72

### X.

STATEMENT MADE BEFORE SUB-COMMITTEE No. 2 OF THE COMMITTEE ON BANKING AND CURRENCY (A BILL TO PROTECT AND SUPPORT CREDIT, 130–151) . . . . . 98

### XI.

THE COMPLETION OF THE NATIONAL BANKING SYSTEM . 152

### XII.

FIXED AND REDEEMABLE CURRENCY . . . . . . . . 159

### XIII.

THE PHILOSOPHY OF THE HISTORY OF BANK CURRENCY IN THE UNITED STATES . . . . . . . . . . . . 178

### APPENDIX.

STATEMENTS OF THE VIEWS OF VARIOUS WRITERS REFERRED TO IN THE PREFACE . . . . . . . . . . 209

INDEX . . . . . . . . . . . . . . . . 231

# PREFACE

THE object of the discussion in this book is to point out the inherent weakness of an ungraded banking system, by which forced liquidations and resulting panic are the legal methods for preserving solvency, and to offer a remedy in a graded system formed by the incorporation of clearing houses under a general federal law with power to issue a clearing house currency, as a means to secure stability and to prevent panics. The effort also is made to show the harmony of a graded system with the political principles of our country.

### CONSIDERATION OF GOVERNMENT CURRENCY EXCLUDED.

No reference is made to the currency of the government, because it is believed that a surplus revenue from an adequate tariff and restriction of expenditures will cure all of its ills. The government is like any corporation or individual having notes outstanding payable on demand. The difference is only in amount, but not in kind. The same rules are applicable to the government as to smaller corporations or to individuals. If the government has a surplus income and a reasonable percentage of its demand obligations in cash on hand, its finances will move along without difficulty.

The constitutional right and power of the government to issue a legal tender currency is sustained by authorities which include President Madison, Daniel Webster, and the Supreme Court of the United States. One at least of the financial writers with whom the framers of the Constitution were familiar used the phrase "to coin paper money," and it is a question whether it cannot be fairly claimed that the words in the Constitution, "to coin money," were not intended to include the power to coin paper money as well as metallic. As a matter of economic and financial policy, the nation is practically a unit in approving the issue of legal tender notes. As a financial measure, the withdrawal of the legal tenders would produce widespread distress and confusion in commercial affairs, and the country could not endure it for a moment. One who believes in the desirability of retirement necessarily has no confidence in the permanence of the ability or willingness of the government to maintain its obligations at par with gold. If he is willing to go to the expense of amassing an additional coin reserve of $200,000,000, and of paying $5,000,000 annual interest on the bonds issued to procure it, his lack of confidence amounts almost to a panic-stricken condition. The country does not share in this solicitude. Confidence has been restored. The endless chain has been started in the other direction, and as long as the present business policy of the government is maintained the greenbacks can cause the country no harm and are a decided benefit. The prevailing feeling is in favor of letting the notes of the government alone. If they were retired with gold and the gold thereafter sent out of the country, there would be a great restriction of business and consequent distress.

### CONFIDENCE RESTORED.

The most serious evil of our present situation is no longer the threatened degradation of our monetary standard. The government's credit has been adequately protected by the sound money victory of 1896, which is to be ascribed to the patriotic assistance rendered to sound money Republicans by sound money Democrats. The business of the country has been put upon a firm basis by a confidence-inspiring tariff, and no further legislation in regard to the nation's finances or obligations is required. Manufactures and general business are beginning again to flourish. Sound money and a protective tariff are the two pillars on which the prosperity of the country rests. Economy should be the foundation stone. The country looks forward to the future with well-founded confidence. Added to these propitious circumstances, a golden shower is falling on our farmers, and upon all who are dependent on them, caused by favoring conditions of trade at home and abroad.

But there is a cloud upon the horizon. It is the diminishing bank reserves. They are drawing near the apprehension minimun. We ask where is the trouble? and every department of business says, It is not in me! We are unerringly guided to see that the trouble is located in that creation of the law which we call our banking system. All business is working smoothly except that. The trouble comes from the fact that everything is protected except banking reserves. All eyes are on them.

We therefore must first inquire, What is our system, and wherein does it differ from others, and what is the cause of the apprehension which exists? All other questions being eliminated by the sound money victory, the passage of the tariff bill, the revival of business and manufactures, and the high prices for farm products, we are able to see what remains to be adjusted. From a business standpoint nothing remains but the banking system.

### DISTINCTION BETWEEN GRADED AND UNGRADED SYSTEMS.

Ours is an ungraded system. An ungraded system is one in which each bank is a counterpart and equal of every other bank. The United States has not reached this system by any haphazard method. It is the result of the orderly development of banking under republican institutions. We will not tolerate a Bank of the United States, nor banks of great capital under special charters with branches in all the States. These methods of banking may thrive under forms of government different from ours, but here they do not thrive, or rather they are not allowed to live. Our political institutions are not compatible with them. But our institutions do allow the existence of a state bank, with branches only within the State, or of individual banks of equal standing before the law, organized under a general law. Under our national banking law, which is the product of our institutions, individual national banks are created, and under state laws individual state banks are likewise. The prevailing characteristic of all the banks of the United States, both state and national, is that they are all of one grade, they are uniform, and therefore ungraded; that is, no banks are higher in grade, or powers, or privileges than any other.

The absence of grade necessitates competition. Each individual bank must take care of itself. There is no provision for mutual support or for united action in an ungraded system. Every bank must make good its reserve within thirty days after notice, under threat of a receivership, and no arrangement is made for assistance. Competition and strife are a necessary sequence of this requirement. Confusion and panic are its results.

Every bank's hand is against its neighbor, and a state of mutually destructive war follows the first appearance of danger. From this prevailing and preëminent characteristic has arisen the more accurately descriptive name of the Competitive system. An ungraded system is necessarily competitive and not coöperative.

A graded system of banks is one which provides a higher order or orders of financial corporations, the grades being distinguished one from another by a difference in powers and functions, and yet united to each other as are courts of law, grades in executive and legislative offices, or rank in the army and navy. We have no difficulty in thinking of grades in connection with these departments, and we know that order, stability, efficiency, coöperation, and peace are secured by their means. Gradation enters necessarily into the idea of any system, and must be established if harmonious interaction is to be secured and competition and strife are to be avoided. A graded system of banks is as necessary for stability and peace in commerce as are superior and inferior courts of law in the ordinary affairs of life; and appeals for aid and counsel are as necessary in one sphere as the other.

Order is said to be Heaven's first law. Gradation introduces order and constitutes a system. Gradation transforms a mob into an army. A graded banking system is a financial army. Its objects are to protect and support commercial credit, that is, the credit of all persons, firms, and corporations engaged in commercial transactions, and to defend the business community from the assaults of distrust and panic. These are the chief objects of the measure advocated in this book. No other banking plan now before the country proposes as its chief end to do this. History and experience show that this protection and support can only be given by a graded banking system.

It is proposed to form this system in our country by the incorporation of clearing houses under a federal law and with federal supervision. Clearing houses are now either voluntary organizations or are incorporated under the laws of the different States in which they are located. Their functions are of vast importance to the community, and federal supervision is a necessity to introduce uniformity and to protect individual banks from arbitrary action.

It is proposed to make the banking system thus constituted a protection and support to the commercial community by giving to the largest clearing houses, at least to one in each State, the power, under proper restrictions, to receive from their bank members, bank assets approved by a loan committee, and issue to them a clearing house currency at seventy-five per cent. of the value of the collateral pledged, receivable at all clearing houses throughout the nation at par.

The result of this system, it is claimed, would be to protect and deliver the country from panics, to equalize interest rates in all sections, and thus to foster and develop foreign and domestic trade and commerce, and promote the welfare of the entire country.

A comparison between graded and ungraded systems is given at length in chapters ii. to vi. inclusive.

### BUSINESS MEN WANT STABILITY.

If a business man is asked what he wants of a banking system, he will reply that, given a uniform measure of value and legal restrictions which will secure prudent bank management, he wants freedom from panics and facility in getting money for legitimate purposes on good collateral at all seasons and in all localities. The one word "stability" will describe all his wants. Stability in the value of the dollar, in the credit of the banks, in the monetary situation, and in the rate of interest. A banking system to be satisfactory to him must assure these advantages. A banking system is created by law to facilitate business. That is its chief object, and incidentally it is supposed that the business of banking will be sufficiently remunerative to attract enough capital to meet the requirements of the public for banking facilities.

If an official bank manager is asked what he

wants of a banking system, he will reply — all provisions which will enable him to make the most profit and the fewest losses and leave him the most free in the management of his bank. His wants are all centred around his interests in his bank. He can bank on any measure of value, he trusts himself and his board for prudent management, he proposes to take care of himself and his bank in any panic, and as to facility in supplying money, he is rather pleased to see rates of interest advance.

From the nature of the case the business man represents the whole country, and the bank manager represents a part of it only.

It is evident that the whole country should have more consideration than a part. A vessel or an implement is made for the use and benefit of the maker, and it should not say to the maker, Why hast thou made me thus?

A banking system is not made primarily for the benefit of banks, but of commerce. "Banks," said Webster, "are made for the borrowers. They are made for the good of the many and not for the good of the few." Care should be taken by legislators to have the business of banking sufficiently profitable, but the first care should be to give the public what they need.

The constitutional power to do this is Congress, and the order in which the subject should be considered, under the overruling guidance of the political principles of our government, is, first, What are the wants of the whole country, its commerce and its business men? and, second, What do the individual interests of the bank require?

To produce a satisfactory system there must be coöperation between three interests, the representatives of the political power, the commerce of the country and its banking interests, each in subordination to the other.

## DEVELOPMENT OF THIS BOOK.

The proposal for a graded system of banks, as discussed in the following pages, was first advanced by the writer during the panic of 1893, under date of July 25th of that year, in the article entitled "The Completion of the National Banking System," which will be found on page 152 of this book.

The conclusions therein stated were arrived at independently, from experience of the troubles then prevailing, and from a conviction that some means must be provided to protect our country from the disasters of constantly recurring panics. A study of methods adopted by the New York Clearing House, in the issue of clearing house certificates, led to the central idea of these pages that clearing houses should be incorporated under a general federal law and brought under government supervision as a prerequisite to the conferring of any powers upon them. By thus constituting them corporate bodies, the national banking system would reach completion. The subject expanded under an investigation, which resulted in the preparation of various articles all leading to the same thought, — the "Carthago delenda est" of this book.

The years which followed 1893 were so disturbed that the investigation never lost its interest and was always timely. Finally in December, 1895, the writer prepared a bill embodying his views, and it was introduced into the House of Representatives, January 7, 1896, as H. R. No. 3338. A hearing before the Committee on Banking and Currency followed, and the preparation of several articles in further explanation and defense of the central idea of incorporation. These various writings have been gathered together in this book, which, therefore, represents and describes the development and growth of a thought which had its rise as a business man's practical suggestion for the relief of business men in a monetary crisis.

#### WORK OF OTHERS IN SAME DIRECTION.

Some reference should be made to the work of others in the same direction, from which it will be seen that experienced writers have suggested that the functions of the clearing house be used, in one way or another, as a means to secure stability in commerce and relief from panics.

In the Appendix will be found statements of the

views of Charles Parsons of St. Louis, Edward Atkinson of Boston, the late Adolph Ladenburg of New York, Hon. Joseph H. Walker of Massachusetts, and others.

T. G.

NEW YORK, January, 1898.

# A GRADED BANKING SYSTEM

## I

### THE SEPARATION OF BANKING FUNCTIONS

ADVOCATED BY DANIEL WEBSTER AND SAMUEL JONES LOYD. — THE RESULT OF THE PANIC OF 1837

WHEN this country was emerging from the panic of 1837, which was caused by the lodgment with individual banks of the power to issue bank notes to circulate as money at the discretion of their boards of directors, Daniel Webster, the greatest statesman and most profound student of bank currency our country has produced, made many speeches on the currency question, both before Congress and on special occasions.

With that catastrophe — the most disastrous of its kind the world has ever seen — before his mind, and seeking a mode for the avoidance of similar occurrences in the future, he said in his speech delivered in Congress on the 17th of March, 1838: "A national bank might be established with more regard to its functions of regulating currency than to its functions of discount."

Methods of regulating the currency were then under discussion in England and the United States;

but Webster's opinion preceded any departure from the model given in 1696 by the formation of the Bank of England.

The separation of the issue of bank currency from other banking functions was first legally enacted in the State of New York by the passage of the free banking law on April 18, 1838. A similar event took place in England in 1844, when the Peel charter of the Bank of England was enacted. The credit of this change is due to Colonel Torrens and Samuel Jones Loyd, a leader in financial discussions. The latter, in his pamphlet published in 1840, shows intimate acquaintance with banking conditions in this country, and quotes Webster's utterances with approval.

The New York law and Peel's charter effected the only radical change in the issue of bank currency made since 1696. The issue of bank currency had always been under the control of the directors of individual banks without exception from 1696 to 1838.

Webster said, as we have seen, that he could conceive of a bank's being organized with more regard to its functions of regulating the currency than its functions of discount. This phrase "to regulate the currency" is now obsolete, and by it was understood merely the rules and methods by which currency is issued and the amount thereof controlled for the promotion of commerce and the prevention of panics. But it is a question whether mere separation of the functions of a bank such as was accomplished in 1838 and 1844 fulfills either Webster's or Loyd's idea. It is evident from S. J. Loyd's writings that he endeavored to incorporate that idea fully in the present Bank charter. "Separate," he wrote to a Manchester merchant, "the management of the circulation, that is, in other words, the power of creating money, from banking business: vest that power exclusively in one body; make all its measures in that capacity perfectly public; let not the borrowers of money — government and commerce — approach with their dangerous and seductive influences the creator of money; but send them where their application ought always to be made, to the subordinate distributers of it; let the manager of the circulation be raised above all reach, and let him thenceforth remain, like the sun in our system, by one never varying influence, regulating, controlling, invigorating everything around him, but himself influenced and moved by none." The New York law of 1838 was also in the same direction. But both the New York law and the Bank charter contain only the beginning, or the half, of Webster's suggestion.

He proposed the formation of a bank to perform the functions of currency issues. A bank means a corporation chartered by law, and fully equipped to transact business of a special character. Neither the New York law nor the Bank charter creates separate corporations to perform the functions of currency issues. They only separate those functions from the other operations of the Bank and provide that they shall be performed by certain officials of the government or of the Bank.

The separation of the function of bank issues was demanded by the great crash of 1837, because when not separated the power had been abused by directors of banks in the United States during the years before 1837, and had been repeatedly abused by the directors of the Bank of England from 1696 to 1844. If the criticism of the directors of the Bank had not been loud and deep, separation could not have been effected. If the losses of 1837 in this country had not been overwhelming, a trusteeship for the currency could not have been established as it was by the New York law of 1838. The separation was a necessity then, and must always continue so under general laws.

It was not merely separation that Webster suggested, but the formation of a bank, or a system of banks, whose only function should be the issue of currency. The whole subject of bank currency would then be not only separated from the control of deposit banks and their individual directors, but confided to other corporations which he conceived might be created for the sole purpose of doing all that is connected with the preparation and issue of bank notes authorized to circulate as money. His idea is not fully realized if separation only is accomplished and the matter handed over to government officials. They do not constitute a bank in any true sense of the word. They constitute a banking department, with routine duties to perform. The officials are limited by law to certain specified acts, and can exercise no discretion in the matter. Their acts are not under the supervision of a board of directors, nor do they have any relation to business or commerce. When banks are established by law to perform the functions of regulating the currency and are limited to that one purpose, then the Websterian idea will be fulfilled. Mere separation does not fulfill it. The same may be said in effect of the suggestions of Samuel Jones Loyd in England.

There are but two dates to remember in the history of bank currency. The first is when the Bank of England was chartered and power was given to its board of directors to issue notes to circulate as money and to hold themselves the security on which the notes were based. The second date is when the New York law was passed in 1838 by which the power to issue currency was separated from the other functions of banks, and banks desiring currency were required to lodge security with a state official as trustee. The rights of the public were then recognized for the first time and an effort was made to protect them. This was the natural outworking of republican principles.

The third and final date will be when under a general federal law the incorporation of banks will be authorized not to do general business, but only to regulate the issue of currency by holding securities pledged by commercial banks and acting as trustees for the public. Then the idea advocated both by Webster and Samuel Jones Loyd will be fully realized.

# II

## A COMPARISON BETWEEN GRADED AND UNGRADED OR COÖPERATIVE AND COMPETITIVE SYSTEMS

### FUNDAMENTAL POLITICAL PRINCIPLES.

THE government of the United States in all its parts is based upon the theories stated in the Declaration of Independence. All the development of our institutions must be in harmony with those theories, and be their legitimate outgrowth. This does not forbid us to enact a law or to adopt a system similar in purpose and effect to one prevailing under any form of government other than our own, but it does require that the law and the system shall be made to conform in their theory and mode of operation to the genius of our institutions. As a result of this practice, if steadily maintained, every part of our government and all the institutions which grow up under it would be made parts of an harmonious whole. In this way only can a government by the people and for the people be intelligently constructed and fairly tested.

These sentiments are now generally accepted throughout our country, and they explain the jealousy which exists of any proposal to adopt foreign methods or follow monarchical examples. This jealousy is well founded, because most of the suggestions of foreign ideas come from those who have an ill-concealed lack of faith in republican institutions, which amounts almost to a desire to see them fail. From the beginning of our government to the present time there has been an "eternal vigilance" over insidious attempts to foist un-American ideas upon us, by which such encroachments have been resisted.

### EXPERIENCE OF OTHER COUNTRIES.

Foreign methods, on the other hand, may be examined with an impartial spirit to find what is good in them, for the purpose of engrafting that good upon our system. This has been done by all our statesmen, beginning with those who composed the convention for the preparation of the Constitution of the United States in 1788, down to the Monetary Commission a hundred years later. It would be an unreasoning prejudice, and one ignorant of the history of the growth of our government, which would object to examining any subject in the light of the experience of foreign nations or which would refuse to recognize the advantages which those nations may have had to aid them in arriving at their conclusions.

### OPINION OF THE CHAMBER OF COMMERCE, PARIS, FRANCE.

For instance, the Chamber of Commerce of Paris, France, has placed upon record, before the Commission appointed in 1864 to examine into the management of the Bank of France, its opinion that "it is from England and the United States that come the beginnings of financial panics." This is too formal a statement to be ascribed to prejudice. It is also one easy of verification or disproof. If by an examination into the history of panics the opinion of the Chamber of Commerce of Paris is sustained, then it becomes necessary to know the causes which make the great English-speaking nations, England and America, more liable to commercial failures and financial panics than the rest of the civilized world. Why should they be the storm areas from which originate the financial blizzards which burst out so frequently upon the world's commerce? Why should a Rothschild say that "France is in a good situation. There is no country in the world where business affairs are more solidly established, or where failures are less numerous"?

It concerns us in this country to examine this matter without prejudice, and to learn what causes the stability of Continental and the instability of English and American finances. If the facts can be discovered and stated, then the question will arise, Can we not modify our system in accordance with our traditions and institutions so as to place our finances upon a basis equally stable with that of any country in the world? If it is a matter of legislation only, the country would look to Congress to pass the necessary laws to reach this end. The bitter financial experience of the past few years has made our country ripe for the adoption of a maturely considered measure based upon and justified by experience.

## STABILITY THE FIRST REQUISITE OF A CREDIT SYSTEM.

It must be premised that stability is the first requisite and chief excellence desired by commerce and trade, and financial panic is the great evil which all wish to avoid. All the business of the civilized world is conducted on the credit system. That is, all sales and purchases are not settled for with an equal amount of coin. Only balances are paid in coin. The adoption of this principle means the adoption of the credit system. By stability is meant the orderly working of the credit system, and by panic, its breaking down.

The chief agency by which credit operations are conducted are the banks, and their ability to pay their circulating notes and deposits on demand at all times in gold is the first condition of stability. The second condition of stability is the ability of the banks to sustain at all times the commerce of a nation in a state of quiet and freedom from monetary panic by supplying the legitimate needs of commerce with loans of money at uniform and reasonable interest charges. Stability describes the condition of commerce and trade when the banks are able to meet all demands upon them both for cash and discounts. If stability can be maintained, then business transactions can be undertaken, based upon the sure ground that no financial disturbance need be anticipated, and the only question to be considered would be the safe and remunerative employment of capital.

The maintenance of stability is no small undertaking, because the credit system has become universal, and obligations and commercial transactions are many times greater than they would be on a basis of barter, which is the strictly cash basis.

The general prosperity is so much increased by the activity of business which results from the credit system, that the maintenance of its stability or orderly working is the most important desideratum in commerce. The problem is, how to maintain credit with the relatively small amount of cash needed to settle balances, and thus avoid the loss which would result from keeping on hand a larger amount of idle capital in the shape of superfluous cash reserves.

### RESTRICTION, EXTRA LEGAL MEASURES, SUSPENSION.

It must further be premised that a banking system may be said to break down when, under financial pressure, banking accommodations are withdrawn and cash payments are either restricted or suspended. In order to maintain the stability which is the first requisite of the credit system, a great struggle will take place before the effort is abandoned, and recourse will be had either to measures provided by the laws on which the banking system is founded, or to some outside of the law, or to a suspension of the law itself.

Experience shows that the measures provided by the laws of the United States and England are not adequate to maintain the orderly working of the credit systems of those countries under financial pressure. The history of commerce in the United States is sufficient to prove the statement as far as it applies to this country. No business man will care to deny it. Panics have become the common experience and business has been ravaged by them to the point of prostration. The experience of England will be referred to later on.

When legal methods for controlling panics and producing stability are ineffective, recourse must be had to extra legal measures, or to a suspension of the laws on which the banking system is founded, in order to prevent a cataclysm. When this alternative takes place, the banking system may be said to break down.

### CREDIT SHOULD BE SUSTAINED BY LEGAL METHODS.

Conversely, a banking system may be said to prove its merit, if it finds within the law of its being all the resources, expedients, and provisions needed to carry it through the severest strains without derangement of its functions or disturbance of the finances of the business community it serves. The banking systems of France and Germany have maintained the stability of commerce in those countries for so many years, that they may fairly claim to answer in the fullest degree these requirements.

### NO REFERENCE HERE TO GOVERNMENT FINANCES.

It must be further premised that we are confining our attention to commercial banking and not to issues of currency by the government, which is an entirely distinct subject.

The money of the government is fixed, and it is to be assumed that it can be kept at par with gold. If so, the notes of the government are equal to a metallic currency, and form the basis on which commercial transactions are conducted. If they are not convertible into gold at par, it is the duty of the government to reduce the amount, or to increase the coin reserves until they are. It is a proper function of the government to provide a paper currency in so far as it is maintained on an equality with gold. The suggestion that the government should go out of the banking business comes from a confusion of ideas and has no reason in it. It is not banking to provide a metallic currency, or one equal to a metallic currency, any more than it is to issue bonds and pay interest.

It is the duty of the government to coin money, and in early writers we meet with the expression "to coin paper money." When a government is in debt it is a wise economic measure to coin as much paper money as can be kept on a par with gold. It is a mode of borrowing without interest, which the government can legitimately avail itself of. There is no principle of law, morals, political economy, or commerce, which can be raised as an objection to a government paper currency when maintained on a par with gold. The only objection is in the liability to over-issue, which is a temptation to which governments have too often succumbed with disastrous consequences. The people of the United States had this temptation presented to them in the last presidential campaign, and they overcame it by an emphatic majority. They have determined that they will not sanction over-issues and will maintain the government currency at a par with gold. That question need no longer be considered.

The limit of the subject we are now attempting to discuss is the consideration of commercial banking operations which are conducted by citizens and corporations under the laws and in the money provided by the government.

### WHY DO FINANCIAL PANICS TAKE THEIR RISE IN ENGLAND AND THE UNITED STATES?

We are now ready to consider the question why financial panics take their rise in the United States and England; for that they do is an historical fact which it is presumed will not be disputed. Reserving the discussion as to the United States, an outline statement comparing the English, French, and German systems of banking becomes necessary, with special and exclusive reference to the orderly working of the credit system in those countries.

# III

## THE ENGLISH SYSTEM

### ENGLISH COMMERCIAL HONOR THE MODEL OF THE WORLD.

The dominant position which the British Empire has so long held in the commerce of the world makes it easy to assent to the opinion expressed by Lord Liverpool and the Chancellor of the Exchequer, F. J. Robinson, in a paper dated 13th of January, 1826, in which they said, "We believe that much of the prosperity of the country [England] for the last century is to be ascribed to the general wisdom, justice, and fairness of the dealings of the Bank of England."

With any criticism that may be made on English banking must be coupled a tribute of respect for the sterling integrity which has been the foundation of British supremacy and has made her commercial honor the model of the world.

### ENGLAND'S FINANCIAL SYSTEM FAILS UNDER SEVERE TEST.

The richest country in the world and the country with the largest and most active commerce, and the country which can compare its thinkers favorably with men of the same class in any other nation, would be expected to have the best banking system that experience and ingenuity could devise. But the very tenacity which has made its success attainable has led England to hold on to its pounds, shillings, and pence, and to defective or antiquated methods which even her own financial authorities have long criticised. England's banking system is among these, for when it is put to the test of a severe panic, it is found to contain no provision to carry the country through its difficulties, and the alternative is presented of either the bankruptcy of the nation on the one hand, or on the other a recourse to expedients contrary to or not contained in its Bank's charter. These expedients are either the suspension of the charter, or a recourse to volunteer methods to ward off the threatened disaster.

### RELIEF FROM SUSPENSION.

The suspension of the Bank's charter is evidently a confession of its inadequacy, but not more so than a recourse to volunteer financiering. If the system were perfect, it would have within itself the provision to meet a panic. But in 1847, three years after the grant of the Bank's charter, in 1857, and in 1866, three crises occurred, in each of which it became apparent that if the enforcement of the charter of 1844 was persisted in, the business community of England would be ruined. Very wisely in each instance the Ministry advised the directors of the Bank of England to disregard the law and save the people, promising an act of indemnity. No sooner was suspension announced on each of these three occasions than the money stringency "vanished like a dream." The public excitement was immediately calmed, and the panics were abated.

### RELIEF FROM VOLUNTEER METHODS.

In 1890, when the Baring panic occurred, a volunteer movement was undertaken to save the country. Under the leadership of the Bank of England a fund of $75,000,000, to guarantee the Baring indebtedness, was pledged, and a loan of $25,000,000 was effected with the Bank of France and other European banks. A volunteer movement is better than a suspension of the charter, but it means that there is no provision in the law establishing the banking system of England to accomplish the desired end, and that some outside expedient or help must be resorted to. This is as much a confession of its inadequacy as a suspension of the Bank's charter.

### NO LEGAL RELIEF EXCEPT BY FORCED LIQUIDATIONS.

The reason for these break-downs of the English banking system is that the Bank of England has no power beyond its cash reserves to protect itself, much less the banks of England, at any serious juncture, except by forcing liquidations upon the business community. When the bank begins thus to protect itself, it inaugurates a panic. All other banks, bankers, and individuals in England must do the same, for they are all organized on the same principle as individual banks, each relying upon its reserves and each competitive with all the others in a time of panic. The panic increases until the point of exhaustion is reached, and then an abandonment of the theory on which the English banking system is founded brings relief.

### CASH RESERVES INADEQUATE.

The Bank cannot issue circulating notes except on a small amount of public securities and on a deposit of bullion. These deposits of bullion form its cash reserves, and are its only resource to meet a demand from depositors. But the reserves are only a fractional part (about 50 per cent.) of the obligations of the Bank, and yet these obligations are relied on by other banks and bankers for their reserves. So it is always in the power of its creditors to give it trouble by demanding payment in gold of their deposits, and this power is multiplied because the deposits are the reserves of other banks. When that contingency arises, its only means of maintaining its reserves is by forcing payments from its debtors. This course always aggravates a panic when it has begun, and sometimes the first step in a panic is taken by the Bank itself.

### ENGLISH THEORY OF RESERVES.

The theory of the English reserve is that it is sufficient to meet any ordinary demands, and during the interval which it affords, time is secured to collect funds from maturing bills receivable and loans to make good any inroads therein. The difficulty with this theory is that all the bank's obligations are on demand, while only the reserve part of its assets is immediately available. When a panic arises, a great deal more than the reserve is immediately wanted. If there is but the reserve between the community and a disastrous liquidation, the state of the reserve becomes the most important factor in the business situation, and a continual source of anxiety. How to manage the reserve, or how to keep it up, becomes a question of vital interest.

### WALTER BAGEHOT ON "THE APPREHENSION MINIMUM."

Walter Bagehot ably discusses the subject in his book on Lombard Street, and says, page 322: "There is a certain minimum which I will call the apprehension minimum, below which the reserve cannot fall without great risk of diffused fear." "The Bank reserve, then, ought never to be reduced below the apprehension point. The only practical mode of obtaining this object is to keep the actual reserve always in advance of the minimum apprehension reserve." How, forsooth, would Mr. Bagehot do this? He does not describe the method, but it is evident that the only way under the English system is by restricting discounts, even at the risk of forcing a panic. The alternatives are to suspend the system or to adopt volunteer methods.

# A STANDING MENACE 19

When this dilemma presents itself, the country is on the verge of a panic, if not already in one.

### PROFESSOR BONAMY PRICE ON RAISING RATE OF DISCOUNT.

Professor Bonamy Price of Oxford can only suggest as a means of controlling a crisis and protecting the reserve to raise the rate of bank discount. This must be immediately recognized as a totally inadequate method. A financial panic is sudden and acute; the effect of raising the bank discount rate would be felt only gradually.

### THE EXPANSIVE METHOD GIVES RELIEF.

MacLeod presents the true view in his "Theory of Credit," when he argues in favor of the expansive mode of controlling panics as opposed to the restrictive. This is the method advocated in the Bullion Report of 1810, and we shall see that it is the guiding principle of French and German finance, when those systems are described. But there must be a legal power to expand as a condition precedent, and this the English system lacks.

The English banking system is therefore a standing menace to the peace of the commercial world. It has no legal way of saving itself except by destroying others, and the volunteer method is a very uncertain reliance.

Manifestly the reserve is entirely inadequate for the purpose, and some large provision, by which at least fifty or one hundred million pounds in undoubted circulating notes could be immediately available, is needed to insure the orderly working of British finances under any and all circumstances.

### CREDIT CURRENCY NEEDED.

A simple and adequate relief could be provided by an act of Parliament giving to the Issue Department of the Bank of England authority and power to issue to any bank under government supervision circulating notes on pledge of commercial assets at a safe percentage of their value. All banks should then be required to receive these notes at their counters at par. If this authority had been in existence in 1847, 1857, and in 1866, there would have been no suspensions of the Bank charter in those years, and in 1890 there would have been no " begging of outside banks and firms to subscribe to a Baring guarantee fund, and no jeering and gibing and mocking at the Bank of England for having to be taken in tow by the Bank of France." (MacLeod.) The machinery would have been ready to meet even the strain of the Baring failure, and to liquidate their enormous indebtedness without disturbance to the commercial world.

### THE ENGLISH BANKING SYSTEM NOT A GOOD MODEL.

The English banking system, therefore, does not present to this country a model worthy of imitation. Its defects are too apparent. As it stands it is a system of competitive banks, every one of which in a panic must strengthen itself from an insufficient coin reserve at the expense of the community and of the other banks. There is no central power to sustain the banks of England in an emergency, and no means of replenishing or protecting reserves except by borrowing in Continental money centres or by producing financial distress at home.

The safety of the English system lies in the immense amount of collateral security centred in London, and in the convenient fact that Paris, where it may be used, is only a few hours distant.

The answer to the question why financial panics take their rise in England is that English banks are competitive, and English laws do not provide any way to support and protect commerce and trade from sudden failures of confidence, except by an inadequate reserve with its apprehension minimum. When such a lack of confidence prevails, English banks, from the Bank of England down, must strengthen themselves at the expense of the community and each other. A panic means an internecine struggle in which every man's hand is against his neighbor, and the signal which precipitates it is the decline of the Bank's reserve to the apprehension minimum. The real question to answer is, how panics could not take their rise in England under such a system.

## IV

### THE FRENCH SYSTEM

#### ITS TWO FUNDAMENTAL THOUGHTS.

WHEN in 1848 the Chamber of Deputies established the Bank of France in its present form, they "cut the Gordian knot without untying it." In the turmoil of a political revolution and a commercial crisis there was no opportunity for calm deliberation over financial questions. Two considerations governed. During the discussion M. Clapier expressed one; he said: "To wish to constitute in France a vast establishment of credit destined to cover with its branches the entire country is a thought which lacks neither *éclat* nor grandeur. This thought flatters at first sight the love of centralization and of unity whose influence dominates all spirits, and which forms the distinctive feature of French institutions." The decree establishing the Bank upon its present foundation expressed the other. It reads: "The essential interests of the country imperiously demand that every bank bill declared to be legal money shall be able to circulate equally in all parts of the land."

#### NOT A MONOPOLY.

The first consideration is the glory of France, and the second, the commercial interests of that country. The Bank of France stands as the embodiment of these two ideas. It has been called a monopoly, as if that was one of its prominent features; but it is not a monopoly in the sense that it was originated for the purpose of enriching a few. The Bank of France has never had that taint upon it. It was established as a governmental institution, and as such was given certain exclusive privileges, but only for the purpose of strengthening and glorifying France. All governments are based upon the reservation of exclusive rights and duties, and the sole performance of special functions for the good of all.

PRIVILEGES AND REGULATIONS OF THE BANK OF FRANCE.

The Bank of France has always been managed for the public good, and should no more be considered as a monopoly than are police officers and boards of health. The privileges granted to it were only a means to the end, and whatever was needed was freely granted by the deputies in the decree establishing the Bank. "This was," said M. Léonce de Lavergne, "a revolutionary act, accomplished without examination, without discussion, without control, only by the good pleasure of the provisional government." The interests of the departments were subordinated to the country, and the rights of the provincial banks were unceremoniously taken from them and concentrated in the Bank of France.

Governmental supervision was established by the

right of the government to appoint the governor and deputy governor of the Bank.

Solidity and credit were secured by the large capital of the Bank. Conservative management was provided by strict rules limiting advances and the use of the funds of the Bank to short three-name paper or collateral security; but the chief and essential feature which distinguishes the Bank of France among the banks of the world is the privilege of issuing circulating notes up to a limit which has been gradually increased until it is now proposed to fix it at $1,000,000,000. All the other characteristics of the Bank may be paralleled in other great national banks, but in this one fact the Bank of France stands without a superior or an equal. It is therefore to this one point that we will direct our inquiries, and for the further reason that this is the subject we are at present investigating.

### LARGE RESERVE MAINTAINED WITHOUT LEGAL REQUIREMENT.

There are two facts regarding this note issue to be remarked: one is, the Bank is not required by law to keep in its vaults any specified percentage of reserve of coin; and the other, that it nevertheless does maintain a coin reserve of about 82 per cent. of its note issues, or 68 per cent. of its total obligations. This enormous store of coin the Bank is free to use at any time to sustain the commerce of France, with no restriction or regard to any ratio of the reserve to obligations. The amount of this coin reserve is in round numbers $600,000,000. It is so far in excess of any ordinary commercial demand for money that rates of discount vary only slightly from one year to another. This overshadowing fact reveals the secret of the stability of French finances.

### SIMPLICITY.

We have here the French system, which is as simple as one can be made. Above all local, private, incorporated, or branch banks, there is the Bank of France, under government supervision, with large capital, with exclusive right of note issues, with 82 per cent. of those issues on hand in coin, and yet with no restrictions to keep any definite percentage of reserves, and therefore with power to use its coin at any time to sustain the commerce of France. It is easy to see why interest rates in France are more uniform than elsewhere, with such a great reserve on guard to aid and protect legitimate business. The knowledge that $600,000,000 are available for instant use is sufficient to protect French commercial credit and to sustain it under any shock, and revive industry even after prostration as complete as that which followed the war of 1870.

### A LARGE RESERVE AT NO COST OF INTEREST.

The thriftiness of French banking is shown in the fact that the maintenance of this reserve is at no cost of interest to the Bank of France. Its entire reserve is provided by its note circulation. By the process of receiving gold on deposit, or buying it, and when called on for cash tendering in payment of such demands silver or its notes, it gradually has supplied all France with the entire circulation needed for home use, and is itself the custodian of an almost equal amount of gold and silver coin.

### BENEFITS OF THE LARGE RESERVE.

The good results of the large reserve of the Bank of France are shown by its history. Since 1848, when it was established with its present privileges, French monetary affairs have moved on with so little disturbance that its financial history is like the uneventful records of a nation at peace. There have been commercial crises in France, such as the catastrophe of the Panama Canal and the collapse of the copper syndicate in 1888, and political crises, such as the German war of 1870 and the period of the payment of the indemnity in 1871, but the banking system of France has not been overthrown by any of them, and has earned its right to the admiration of the world by its steadiness under the severest strain, and by acting as the most potent agency in bringing about the revival of the productive industry of France, after the German war of 1870 and the restoration of specie payments in 1877. All these results come not only from its large reserve, but from the power to use it at will to sustain the commerce of France. The power of the Bank is therefore enormous, and far beyond any demands except those which might arise during war.

### ARGUMENTS FOR DEPARTMENTAL BANKS.

It is well to recall the discussion in the Chamber of Deputies in 1848, that we may know that even then the local issue of currency had its strong defenders. M. Clapier said, " From the commercial point of view the departments had a just subject of alarm when they saw the fate of their commerce and their industry bound entirely to that of a single establishment." M. Léon Faucher said that the departmental banks "had the courage to found institutions of credit in cities when the first efforts of the Bank of France had failed. They had grouped the local resources and had commenced to awaken the spirit of association outside of the capital." "The branches of the Bank of France," he said, "have no roots in the localities which they serve, they are not to the manner born (*ils n'y sont pas nés*), they are unmistakable colonies from the metropolis. They do not use the influence which might bring them local business, which is, I think, one of the principal causes of their inferiority." M. Faucher drew a conclusion in favor of a system which should make of departmental banks a sort of confederation. It is in this discussion that "the last word of the government on the question of the departmental banks must be found," but the debate ended by the establishment of the Bank of France in its simplicity and in its strength. It was a war measure, and, like a fortress, the ability to withstand financial shocks was the first requisite.

## COMPARISON OF ENGLISH AND FRENCH SYSTEMS.
### NO COMPETITION IN FRANCE.

The first difference between the English and French systems is shown by this discussion to be the competition between English banks and the entire absence of competition between French banks. The effect of a panic in England is, as we have seen, to start a struggle between all banks, institutions, and firms for gold and currency. A money panic can hardly occur in France, because if a demand arises from depositors, the bank on which the run is made would immediately apply to the Bank of France for a re-discount, and the run would be stopped. French banks, therefore, are not competitive, because they can get assistance from a bank which occupies a higher grade than they, and application to which is no discredit.

### BANK OF FRANCE SUSTAINS ALL FRENCH BANKS.

In fact, as proof of solvency and strength, a local French bank will advertise its condition, showing that it has 10 per cent. of its liabilities on hand in cash, 10 per cent. in call loans, and 50 per cent. in "bills receivable immediately discountable at the Bank of France." Such a position is impregnable. Thus the strength and credit of the Bank of France are imparted to all the banks of the nation.

#### A GRADED SYSTEM ABOLISHES COMPETITION AND PANIC.

There can be no competition between banks which are graded. The Bank of England lacks the essential requisite to enable it to be at the head of English banks, that is, it has no power to render assistance in time of need by the issue of credit currency, but must either go to the Bank of France or to other money lenders for help, or suspend its charter. It must enter into competition for gold with all the other banks of England, with which, in that particular, it is on a level.

So the chief characteristic of the French system is that it is graded. The Bank of France completes the system, because it is of a grade higher than all other French banks. It not only has greater capital and is under government supervision, but it has superior powers not enjoyed by the lower. Owing to its higher position and powers it can be appealed to for aid, and its large reserve enables it to grant assistance wherever needed.

The lesson we can learn from French finance is the benefit of a large available reserve.

#### AVAILABLE RESERVE VS. THE CURRENCY PRINCIPLE.

The English and French systems differ, secondly, in the relations of their banks to the reserve. The Bank of France is entirely free from any restriction in its management of its reserve or of its note issues. The Bank of England is compelled to cancel its notes as its coin reserves decline. The French method holds its entire mass of coin ready to sustain the commercial community in time of panic; the English method creates panic, aggravates it, and sacrifices its business community on the mistaken theory, which is the foundation of Peel's bill, called the "currency principle," that "when bank notes are permitted to be issued they should exactly equal the gold they are alleged to displace, and that for every five sovereigns drawn out of the bank, a five-pound note should be withdrawn from circulation."[1] The frequent break-downs of the English system and the stability of the French system under severe strain prove conclusively two points; first, that the so-called currency principle produces panic, and second, that the opposite principle of an available reserve produces stability. The "currency principle," with competitive banks, is the English; the available reserve, with graded banks, is the French. Looking over the ramparts of their enormous reserve, the Frenchmen were right in saying: "*C'est d'Angleterre et des Etats-Unis, où existe la pluralité des banques, que viennent les commencements de crise.*"

[1] MacLeod, *Theory of Credit*, p. 687.

# V

## THE GERMAN SYSTEM

### UNLIMITED POWER OF ISSUE.

"THE distinguishing novelty of the German law," says Professor Dunbar, "is the power given to increase the uncovered issue beyond the limit (of 385,000,000 marks) subject to payment of the tax of five per cent., in order to secure a certain degree of elasticity at the point where, under the English law, the rigidity of the line drawn by Peel's act has sometimes presented a frightful dilemma. This elastic limit has several times taken effect in the case of the smaller banks and also in the case of the Reichsbank in December, 1881, in September and October, 1882, in December, 1884, in January, 1885, in December, 1886, and three times in the latter part of 1889, the issues of the bank being in some of these cases to a considerable amount beyond the fixed limit. On more than one occasion it seems certain that the operation of the elastic provision was successful in saving the German community from what would have been a severe spasm of contraction under the usual administration of Peel's act."

## OTHER PROVISIONS.

The German system was formed in 1875, and is consequently the most recent of the great banking systems of the world, and coming into existence with the establishment of the empire, an opportunity was given to use the world's experience untrammeled by customs and precedents. "In a part of this system are easily traceable the general outline of the English Bank Charter Act of 1844," says Professor Dunbar. Charles A. Conant writes: "Those banks which were not disposed to accept the new conditions were dealt with in a manner similar to the French departmental banks after the revolution of 1848." The connection of the government with the Imperial Bank of Germany is similar in many respects to the model of the Bank of France. A general circulation of notes was provided after the means used in Scotland, Prussia, and Switzerland, by obliging the different banks to mutually exchange their bills, a provision which existed in the State Bank of Indiana and in other state systems in the United States.

### SPECIAL POWERS CONFERRED ON A FEW BANKS.

All these provisions present no new features, but in the power given to the Imperial Bank and the six other banks of issue to increase their note issues *ad libitum* a radical departure was made from all established precedents. This "novelty," as it is called, is the provision which relates to the subject we are investigating, and we can therefore confine our attention exclusively to that.

## TWO ADVANTAGES — PROTECTION TO BANKS, SUPPORT OF COMMERCIAL CREDIT.

The legal privilege granted to the Imperial Bank and to a few other banks which form a grade higher than popular banks of issuing their notes without limit, should be considered in two aspects. First, as a reserve power to protect the banks of issue against sudden demands; second, as a means of sustaining the credit and facilitating the business of the commercial community of Germany.

### PROTECTION TO BANKS.

The law of 1875, establishing the German system, says in effect that the ordinary rule shall be that the banks of issue shall hold in cash a reserve of $33\frac{1}{3}$ per cent. of their total circulation, but as extraordinary demands are likely to occur, the banks of issue may put out additional notes without limit, but on such excess of uncovered notes a tax of 5 per cent. per annum shall be imposed. The theory is that such excess of issues is objectionable and might be a source of danger to the banks; and therefore a tax should be imposed thereon sufficiently heavy to prevent their issue, unless the demand for money were acute. But as a perfect system must contain within itself the means of self-defense, the objections to an unlimited issue are overbalanced by the necessity of self-preservation.

The provision for unlimited issues is conferred only on the Imperial Bank and six others. It would evidently enable them to liquidate all their demand obligations if pushed to an extreme. It is a perfect protection against runs or panics, and the result is that monetary panics do not take their rise in Germany. Imagine the German banks operated on the principle prevailing in England and the United States, and dependent only on their gold reserve of $33\frac{1}{3}$ per cent., and it can be asserted without fear of contradiction that panics would occur under such circumstances. This provision, then, acts the same as a reserve in cash of 100 per cent. of liabilities. It is merely a legal reserve power and costs nothing to maintain.

### THE RESERVE POWER OF THE HIGHER GRADE OF BANKS PREVENTS PANICS.

The solidity of the German system, without a monetary panic for over twenty years, proves to us that a reserve need not be in the shape of gold and silver, as in the case of the Bank of France, but that it is equally serviceable and effective if it is in bank assets against which the law permits an issue of notes: also that the reserve need not be held by one bank, but may be distributed among several. It is a reserve power rather than an actual reserve. The two systems of France and Germany agree in this, that they each provide a large fund which is available to the banks of those countries to meet any sudden demand. In France the fund is in the gold and silver held by the Bank of France, which it has obtained by the issue of its notes. In Germany the fund is in the assets of the Imperial Bank and a few other large banks against which they are authorized to issue their notes. The banks of lower grade of both countries are thus protected by a fund provided by law to carry them over any monetary panic; consequently in neither country do they have monetary panics, and this is only due to the legal provision of a large available reserve.

### ALL NOTES MUST BE RECEIVED AT PAR BY EVERY BANK OF ISSUE.

There are but few banks of issue in Germany, and it is therefore possible to require " every bank of issue to receive at par the notes of every other bank." This places where it rightfully belongs the guarantee of the goodness of the circulating medium, that is, on the concerns which derive a profit therefrom.

" The credit of the notes is maintained," says Professor Dunbar, " by their strict convertibility and by the law which makes them everywhere current in payments to any bank of issue." These facts prove to us from the German system what has already been deduced from the French, that it is the available reserve which produces stability, and it matters not in what form it is provided, whether it is lodged in a single bank or is a power conferred upon many, but in either case the banks of issue must be of a higher grade than the popular banks.

We have thus considered the first of the two aspects of this legal reserve power.

### SUPPORT OF COMMERCIAL CREDIT.

The second is its relation to sustaining and protecting the credit and commerce of Germany. The few banks of issue in Germany constitute a class or grade higher than the many credit institutions which are nearer the people. The great Imperial Bank has its 276 or more branches. There are many banking institutions and popular coöperative banks also. The members of the last-named class number over half a million persons. They form, says Professor Jannet, "a hierarchy of banks, which by the successive re-discount of their paper cause the bills of exchange of the most modest artisans to reach the Imperial Bank." The German system, like the French, therefore, provides a system of graded banks, and at the head are the banks which have the power of unlimited issue. These are under government supervision and have the confidence of the people equally with the government. In a graded system there can be no competition for coin between banks of the lower or popular grade, and there is no competition in Germany. If an emergency arises, relief can be obtained through discounts which find their way up from the lower to the higher banks. No use of money is safer than re-discounting discounted bills, with the addition to the original security of the name of the lower bank as an additional indorser. Commercial credit is sustained and protected by a system which thus provides an infallible way of obtaining discounts in time of need. The German system is not so strong as the French, but its differences illustrate the mechanism of a reserve, and show us that stability is only a matter of legal enactment.

# VI

## THE UNITED STATES SYSTEM

### A COMPETITIVE SYSTEM LIKE THAT OF ENGLAND.

An examination of the banking system of the United States shows that in essential particulars it is similar to that of England. Its distinguishing characteristic is that our federal and state laws provide for a multiplicity of individual competitive banks, with a reserve provided out of the cash resources of the bank as a protection against insolvency and panic. No power of note issue is given except on security of government bonds. The legal method of protecting reserves is the restrictive, that is, enforcing liquidations of bank assets. These characteristics make our system like the English, and for these reasons panics of the same kind prevail in both countries. All the defects of the English system are therefore experienced in the United States. When the reserves of our banks are encroached upon by demands from depositors, so that they are brought near the apprehension minimum, or more often when it is thought necessary by bank officials to make provision for anticipated demands, it becomes the duty of the banks, and it is their only legal mode of relief, to demand payment of loans and discounts irrespective of the effect on borrowers or on market prices. This is also the English method.

### THE APPREHENSION MINIMUM PRODUCES CONSTANT ANXIETY.

The apprehension that such liquidation may be demanded at any time produces a constant state of anxiety in the business community. The withdrawal of bank accommodation from merchants and others in a spasmodic way without reason, except that the banks have no other recourse, paralyzes business, retards the development of the country, and produces hard times. No calculations as to the money market are possible, and the chance of a panic must always be taken into consideration by business men. Rates of interest cannot be uniform, and the spasms of liquidation cause not infrequently extravagant charges for money.

The maintenance of the reserve becomes therefore a subject of perpetual solicitude to bank managers, and when the reserve declines at the great money centres all the business community is disturbed, for it is well understood that the banks are unable to conform to the requirements of the law, except by compelling sacrifices by the borrowing public. This being the only recourse of the banks, the condition of bank reserves is the one important question in United States finance.

## APPREHENSION JUSTIFIED BY SMALLNESS OF RESERVES.

That this state of apprehension is well founded, and that these disturbances are not without cause, is proved by the small percentage of reserve to liability held by the banking institutions of the United States.

From the statistics contained in the Report of the Comptroller of the Currency of December 17, 1896, it appears that on October 6, 1896, the average cash reserves of the different classes of banks in the United States were the following percentages of their demand obligations: —

|   |   | Deposits. | Cash Reserve. | Per cent. |
|---|---|---|---|---|
| 3676 | National Banks | $1,798,756,734 | $343,143,362 | 19.07 |
| 3708 | State Banks | 695,659,014 | 101,038,641 | 14.52 |
| 824 | Private Banks | 59,116,378 | 6,157,561 | 10.41 |
| 8208 | Commercial Banks | 2,553,533,026 | 450,339,564 | 17.63 |
| 260 | Loan and Trust Co's. | 586,468,156 | 26,800,871 | 4.56 |
| 988 | Savings Banks | 1,935,466,468 | 35,201,528 | 1.82 |
| 9456 | All banks | 5,075,467,650 | 512,341,963 | 10.09 |

The smallness of the cash reserves carried by loan and trust companies and savings banks, about four and a half per cent. and two per cent. of their deposits respectively, is due to the protection given by the time limit. Loan and trust companies practically do not take advantage of this privilege, but excluding them from the calculation it appears that the average cash reserve of the commercial banks, that is, national, state, and private, compared with their demand obligations, is 17.63 per cent. If the loan and trust companies are included, the percentage would be 15.20, and if the savings banks, 10.09. The business of the country is done ultimately by commercial banks, that is, national, state, and private, and not only does trade and commerce depend upon them, but in a large degree the loan and trust companies and savings banks also. The commercial banks guard the solvency and stability of our finances, and consequently the ratio of their cash reserves to their demand obligations, and the means by which they can protect themselves, become matters of the first consequence to the welfare of our country.

## IS 17.63 PER CENT. A SAFE RESERVE?

The question then is, Is 17.63 per cent. a safe ratio for a cash reserve? The subject of the availability of deposit reserves and a recourse to loans, discounts, and securities is discussed in a subsequent chapter. Experience shows that this amount of cash reserve in lawful money, that is, 17.63 per cent., is too small to insure stability in our finances, and the efforts of the banks to maintain their reserves are attended with disastrous results. In 1893 loans were curtailed by the national banks alone to the extent of $370,000,000, producing calamitous effects from which the country has not yet recovered. This great sacrifice was occasioned because the banks were compelled to pay depositors $298,000,000, and they had no other way to raise the money except by producing a panic and almost ruining the country.

#### DO BANKS BEGIN PANICS?

In all panics it is a question who become frightened first, the banks or the public. There are some shrewd observers, authorities on both English and American finance, who think that the first step in every panic is taken by the banks, who are watching financial events more closely and are more ready to take alarm than the commercial public. But when once the fight is begun, it must go on to a finish.

#### THE ISSUE OF CLEARING HOUSE CERTIFICATES COMPARED TO SUSPENSION AND VOLUNTEER METHODS.

The desperate remedy of the issue of clearing house certificates is an expedient parallel to the suspension of the charter of the Bank of England, or the resort to volunteer methods. The issue of clearing house certificates is a confession of the lack in our banking system of any provision by which a collapse of credit may be avoided. It is an acknowledgment that the reserve provided by law is insufficient to ward off disaster, or that liquidation can be pressed any further without utter ruin to the business community. It is a suspension of the operation of the provisions of the National Banking Act as regards reserves, and it is a resort to a voluntary combination among the members of clearing houses not contemplated in the law. By it the banks agree to pay out their cash reserves and hold in their place clearing house certificates secured by pledge of convertible collateral.

### SUSPENSION OF NATIONAL BANKING ACT.

The adoption of this measure is justified by the gravity of the situation, and by its successful operation. It means that the already small reserves of the banks have been reduced to the danger point, and the requirement of the National Banking Act for their maintenance at the legal limit must be openly and boldly disregarded. The Comptroller of the Currency can easily be induced to wink at this infraction of the law, and the whole country can be asked to submit to the inconvenience of a restriction in cash payments. When any holder of a demand obligation of a bank calls for lawful money, he can be taken into the cashier's room and be subjected to an inquisition as to what he wants it for, and if possible argued out of his request. This state of affairs is equivalent to a suspension of the charter of the Bank of England with a promise of an act of indemnity, and, like suspension, it is remedial and not preventive. It comes after a panic and not before. It means that the apprehension minimum has been passed, and that any remedy, however desperate, is to be preferred to a continuation of enforced liquidations.

### MONETARY CRISIS PRODUCED BY SMALL LOSS OF RESERVES.

From the low state of the reserves it is evident that a slight loss of cash, even as small as five per cent. of deposit liabilities, is sufficient to produce a monetary crisis. This is a very weak condition. The fact that all the assets of the national and other banks are sound does not give relief when there is no money to be had except at a sacrifice. Our condition is similar to that of English banks, but it is more precarious because our money centres are far removed one from the other, and foreign money markets are still more distant.

### ADDITIONAL PROVISIONS NEEDED TO INSURE STABILITY.

Reserves of 17.63 per cent. are not sufficient to produce stability in our country's finances, and we require some provision by which, in case of need, our banks can have an amount of undoubted circulating notes to meet a drain like that of 1893 without prostrating the country. This would place us on a footing of stability equal to that of the French and German nations, and give us the needed protection against the frequent contractive spasms of the money market which have wrought such evil in our country of late years. The difficulty is only with our banking laws, and can be as readily cured in our country as it has been in France and Germany.

If 17.63 per cent. is too small a reserve for competitive banks to carry, then some means must be found to increase the available cash. But it must be recognized that the reserve may not be wanted, therefore it should not be provided by capital withdrawn from productive use. It will cost nothing and will be just as serviceable if it is provided by law as a power which may be used in case of need. A bank will keep a minimum reserve if it is to be provided out of capital which should be earning interest, or out of deposits on which interest is paid. But a bank will keep a maximum reserve if it is provided at no loss to the bank. If the feeling of security costs, the banker will buy it at as low a price as possible. If it is to be had for nothing, he will carry all of it that he can.

### CURRENCY MUST HAVE UNIVERSAL CREDIT AND CONVERTIBILITY.

But no currency should be authorized which the banks themselves will not take at par. If so, the currency must be secured and its prompt payment guaranteed in a way that will make it absolutely safe to any holder. This can be done by creating a grade of banks higher than our ordinary commercial banks to act as trustees for the public. This grade can be made out of our clearing houses, which already perform valuable functions in our banking system. If organized under federal law, they can act for our banks in the same way that the Bank of France and the German banks of issue act for popular French and German banks. By this means our banks would be supplied with a reserve equal to the par of their capital, or six hundred millions of dollars, which would be sufficient to support and protect commercial credit in the United States in any monetary panic, and would probably prevent all panics in the future.

### FEATURES OF A LAW TO INCORPORATE CLEARING HOUSES.

The law incorporating clearing houses should give to one of the number in each State power to receive convertible assets from banks in that State, and issue to them circulating notes thereon at 75 per cent. of their value, to an amount not in excess of their capital, these notes to be guaranteed first by the bank to whom they are issued, then by the associated banks in the clearing houses of its State, and finally by all clearing houses, and these notes to be received at par through any clearing house in the United States.

This will give a currency locally issued of undoubted soundness, which will circulate at par over the entire country. It will avoid banking monopoly, and issues by numerous banks dependent for credit on the solvency of each, but chiefly it will give to our commerce and trade that protection and stability which come from a graded system of banks and an ample available bank reserve. Let our lawgivers provide the banks with a reserve which shall cost them nothing, and make it as large as prudent, so that it may be said of our land that failures are reduced to a minimum, and panics do not arise here.

### PREVAILING DEPRESSION DEMANDS RELIEF.

Our country has, during the past few years, passed through an ordeal which may almost be compared to the effect on France of the German war of 1870. The liquidation which has been forced upon our country has ruined much productive business; our manufactories have been prostrated; our banks have suffered, especially those in the outlying districts where their assistance is most needed; markets for the products of the farm have been taken away; merchants have seen their profits dwindle and disappear; laborers have gone back to other countries because they could not find work here; the poor have complained of hard times; and the development of our country has been greatly retarded and in some respects brought to a standstill.

All banking should be subservient to the interests of the borrowers. They are the bread-winners on whom the prosperity of the land depends. Their capital in business is many times that of all the capital of all the banks.

We now need, if ever in our history, such a service as was rendered by the Bank of France to the French nation after the prostration of the German war of 1870. The Bank then used its great power to set in motion the wheels of industry, and it was this agency more than any other single cause which restored prosperity to France. In the same way our country now should have the support of a perfected banking system that will not turn around and destroy the commerce which it has brought into being because the law provides no other way by which the banks can protect themselves.

Is it not time to abandon the competitive system,

with its disasters and confusion, and adopt a graded one, with its order and stability?

The change from a competitive to a graded system of banking is a radical one. Yet it would not be noticeable to the public because it requires no change in our existing banks or banking methods which other proposed plans necessitate. The National Banking Act, with which we are so familiar, would stand without amendment. The public would only be concerned to know that monetary panics are a thing of the past. The new legislation would have reference only to the incorporation of clearing houses. The change involves no experiment, because a graded system has been in successful operation for many years in some of the old state banking systems of this country, and in large nations of Europe. The details are so simple that all banks could understand and carry them into effect without difficulty. The protecting structure would rise noiselessly over the heads of the people without the sound of axe or hammer.

# VII

## A DISCUSSION OF THE CONDITION OF BANKING RESERVES IN THE UNITED STATES AS THE CAUSE OF OUR FINANCIAL TROUBLES

A SPECIFIC location of the difficulty with the banking system of the United States is needed, like a diagnosis of a disease, so that we may know whether or not a plan proposed as a remedy, whatever it may be, will go to the affected spot and give the desired relief. The difficulty may be located by the aid of statistics.

Our inquiry must first be directed to the condition of the banking reserves. It is on *the condition of the reserves* that the health of the body financial depends. The central principle of the credit system is the maintenance of obligations at par by means of a cash reserve.

A statement of the reserves of all the banking institutions of the country making reports to the Comptroller of the Currency is given on page 40. The following discussion has reference only to national banks, for the reason that the statistics regarding them are given with the greatest fullness by the Comptroller, while statistics relating to state and private banks, loan and trust companies and savings banks, are too fragmentary to admit of satisfactory examination or accurate deductions.

In addition, it is to be remarked that national banks make a stronger showing than state and other banks, and if there is any weakness in the situation of national banks it is indicative of still greater weakness on the part of the rest of our financial institutions. No charge of unfairness can be made to the figures presented, for they give a view, the most favorable possible that can be taken of any class of banks in the United States.

Banking reserves under our national banking law are divided into two classes, reserves in lawful money and deposit reserves. Let us consider first —

### RESERVES IN LAWFUL MONEY.

The figures in the following table are taken from the last report of the Comptroller of the Currency to Congress, in which national banks are divided into three classes, country banks, and banks in reserve cities of the first and second class.[1]

---

[1] A division of States into two classes, 'Bryan' and 'McKinley,' has been adopted in speeches on the currency question before Congress. To some extent that division has been followed here, because the classification is not only political but geographical and historical, and divides the States in some degree according to accumulated wealth. The figures given in the report of the Comptroller, and in other public documents, have been used without any particular attempt to verify or correct them. The statistics are sufficiently accurate to establish the conclusions stated.

# RESERVES OF NATIONAL BANKS

## TABLE I.

*Reserves of National Banks in lawful money, showing percentages thereof to deposits, and surplus percentages above requirements, October 6, 1896.*

| STATES. | | Division in Report of Comptroller. | | Number of banks. | Deposits. | Reserves held in lawful money. | Percentages of reserves held. | | |
|---|---|---|---|---|---|---|---|---|---|
| Bryan. | McKinley. | | | | | | Required per cent. | To deposits. | Above requirements. |
| Col., Nev. | Cal., Or. | 2 | No. 7 | 106 | $43,966,110 | $12,760,391 | 6 | 29.02 | 23.02 |
| N. C., S. C., Ga., Florida, Ala., Miss., Louisiana, Tex., Arkansas, Tenn. | Kentucky | 10 | No. 4 | 466 | 84,684,280 | 15,279,867 | " | 18.04 | 12.04 |
| S. Dak., Idaho, Mont., Utah, Wash., Wyo. | N. Dak. | 6 | No. 8 | 182 | 36,954,766 | 6,339,336 | " | 17.15 | 11.15 |
| Southern and Western States | | | | 754 | 165,605,156 | 34,379,594 | " | 20.76 | 14.76 |
| Mo., Kans., Nebraska | Ohio, Ind., Ill., Mich., Wis. | 5 | No. 5 | 697 | 169,427,366 | 26,752,230 | " | 15.79 | 9.79 |
| | Ia., Minn. | 3 2 | No. 6 | 492 | 67,697,900 | 9,055,803 | " | 13.38 | 7.38 |
| Virginia | Del., Maryland, West Virginia | 1 3 | No. 3 | 135 | 36,600,420 | 4,884,453 | " | 13.35 | 7.35 |
| Middle States | | | | 1,324 | 273,725,686 | 40,692,486 | " | 14.86 | 8.86 |
| | N. Y., N. J., Penn. | 3 | No. 2 | 717 | 251,007,500 | 27,332,649 | " | 10.97 | 4.97 |
| | Me., N. H., Ver., Mass., R. I., Conn. | 6 | No. 1 | 534 | 162,750,540 | 16,382,477 | " | 10.07 | 4.07 |
| Eastern States | | | | 1,251 | 413,758,168 | 43,715,126 | " | 10.61 | 4.61 |
| Bryan States 22 | McKinley 23 | | Total Country Banks | 3,329 | 853,088,942 | 118,987,206 | " | 13.94 | 7.94 |
| Banks in reserve cities of second class in Bryan States | | | | 35 | 45,960,452 | 10,640,134 | 12½ | 23.15 | 10.65 |
| Banks in reserve cities of second class in McKinley States | | | | 234 | 419,561,590 | 72,620,837 | " | 17.31 | 4.81 |
| Total number of banks in reserve cities of second class | | | | 269 | 465,522,042 | 83,260,971 | " | 17.88 | 5.38 |
| Banks in central reserve cities | | | | 78 | 480,145,746 | 140,895,085 | 25 | 29.34 | 4.34 |
| Total reserve banks | | | | 347 | 945,667,788 | 224,156,056 | | 23.70 | 4.85 |
| Total banks in United States | | | | 3,676 | 1,798,756,730 | 343,143,262 | | 19.07 | 6.60 |

## RESERVES A COMMON STANDARD FOR COMPARISON.

In order to compare banking conditions in different parts of our country, a common standard must be adopted and the banks be compared with each other with regard to that. The standard used in the above table is the percentage to demand obligations of cash reserve in lawful money held in the custody of the banks. In this table the divisions are not arranged numerically as in the Comptroller's report, but according to percentage of reserve then held.

### RESERVES OF COUNTRY BANKS.

When the eight divisions comprising 3,329 country banks are compared by this standard, it appears that the 754 country banks in the Southern and Western States hold the largest average percentage of cash reserves, 20.76 per cent. of their demand obligations; the 1,324 country banks of the Middle States the next largest, 14.86 per cent.; and the 1,251 country banks of the Eastern States the lowest percentage, only 10.61 per cent.

### RESERVES OF BANKS IN SECOND CLASS RESERVE CITIES.

Of the 269 banks in reserve cities of the second class, the 35 banks in cities in Bryan States hold a much larger percentage of reserve than the 234 banks in cities in McKinley States, the percentages being 23.15 and 17.31 respectively.

### RESERVES OF BANKS IN CENTRAL RESERVE CITIES.

The 78 banks in central reserve cities are a class by themselves, and hold 29.34 per cent. in lawful

## POWERFUL ELEMENT OF DISTURBANCE 53

money. The average of all banks in reserve cities is 23.70.

### THE WEAK SPOT IS IN COUNTRY BANKS IN THE EASTERN STATES.

If there is any weakness as regards lawful money reserve in the banks thus classified it must be in the 1,251 country banks in the 'McKinley Eastern States' of New York, Pennsylvania, New Jersey, Maine, New Hampshire, Rhode Island, Vermont, and Connecticut, which hold only 10.61 per cent. of cash reserves. These banks with their large deposits bring down the average percentage in lawful money for the whole country to 19.07 of demand obligations. These 1,251 Eastern banks, with only their 10.61 per cent. of cash reserves, form a powerful element to disturb the condition of the Eastern reserve cities at the slightest alarm. This has been noticed in every panic. The example of the so-called 'Bryan States' might be followed with advantage by these 1,251 banks in the Eastern States.

### THE AMOUNT OF LAWFUL MONEY RESERVE HELD ABOVE LEGAL REQUIREMENTS.

The amount of reserve required by the National Banking Act to be held in lawful money by country banks is 6 per cent., by banks in reserve cities of the second class, 12.50 per cent., and by banks in central reserve cities, 25 per cent. Banks must maintain these percentages under penalty of the appointment of receivers. These percentages therefore form a dead line beyond which banks can go only at the peril of their lives, and consequently they all hold, or strive to hold, for safety a margin of lawful money above these requirements. The following statement shows how much reserve in lawful money the national banks have in their own custody above legal requirements, which they are at liberty to use before calling for outside help. The statement is condensed thus: —

TABLE II.

*Surplus lawful money reserves above legal requirements.*

| No. of Banks. | Class. | Deposits. | Cash Reserve. | | Surplus held above legal requirements. |
|---|---|---|---|---|---|
| | | | Required. | Held. | |
| 3,329 | Country banks | $853,088,942 | $48,278,026 | $118,987,306 | $70,709,280 |
| 269 | Reserve cities of second class | 465,522,042 | 57,217,038 | 83,260,971 | 26,043,933 |
| 78 | Central reserve cities | 480,145,746 | 118,877,525 | 140,895,085 | 22,017,560 |
| 3,676 | Total national banks | $1,798,756,730 | $224,372,589 | $343,143,362 | $118,770,773 |

To appreciate the full significance of this statement, a comparison must be made between the total amount of deposits in the 3,676 national banks, when this statement was rendered, which was $1,798,756,734, and the amount of the surplus reserve they held over that required by law, which was $118,770,775. The surplus reserve, therefore, for which they could be called upon by depositors, and could pay out to them without reducing their reserves below the financial dead line, was only 6.6 per cent.

## COMPARISON OF COUNTRY BANKS.

A particular examination of this table in connection with the preceding one is required. When the different classes of country banks are compared with each other, their relative position as to surplus reserve is the same as when the gross cash reserve only was considered. It appears that the country banks in the Southern and extreme Western States, 754 in number, with $165,605,156 of deposits, were in the strongest position, with a surplus reserve in lawful money of 14.76 per cent. above the percentage required by law. The country banks in the Middle States rank next, with their 1,324 banks holding deposits to the amount of $273,725,686. Their surplus in lawful money is 8.86 per cent. The Eastern country banks, 1,251 in number, holding deposits of $413,758,108, held a surplus reserve in lawful money of only four and six tenths (4.6) per cent. As the deposits of the Eastern banks are much the largest, they bring down the average of the total 3,329 country banks, holding $853,088,942 deposits, to a surplus of lawful money reserve of only 7.94 per cent.

## COMPARISON OF BANKS IN RESERVE CITIES.

We will now examine the condition of banks in reserve cities. For the purpose of comparison, the reserve cities of the second class may be divided into 'Bryan' and 'McKinley' cities. It then appears that the 35 banks in cities in Bryan States, with deposits of $45,960,452, had a surplus reserve in lawful money of 10.65 per cent., and the 234 banks in cities in McKinley States, holding deposits of $419,561,590, had a surplus of only 5.81 per cent. As there are but three central reserve cities, they form a single class, with 78 banks holding $480,145,746 deposits and with a surplus reserve in lawful money above the apprehension minimum of 4.34 per cent.

The following gives these percentages in condensed form:—

TABLE III.

*Showing Percentages of Surplus Reserves.*

| Class. | Percentage of lawful money reserve required. | Percentage of lawful money reserve held. | Surplus held over requirements. |
|---|---|---|---|
| | Per cent. | Per cent. | Per cent. |
| Country banks in Southern and Western States | 6 | 20.76 | 14.76 |
| In Middle States | 6 | 14.86 | 8.86 |
| In Eastern States | 6 | 10.61 | 4.61 |
| Average | 6 | 13.96 | 7.94 |
| Reserve banks in Bryan cities of second class | 12½ | 23.15 | 10.65 |
| Reserve banks in McKinley cities of second class | 12½ | 17.31 | 4.81 |
| Reserve banks in central reserve cities | 25 | 29.34 | 4.34 |
| Average of all national banks in United States | | 19.07 | 6.60 |

## COMPARISON OF CONDITION OF EASTERN AND WESTERN BANKS.

Banks in the East and West may be approximately compared as follows: The 1,251 Eastern country banks, the 234 banks in reserve cities of the second class in McKinley States, and the 78 banks in the central reserve cities, making 1,563 banks out of 3,676, hold $1,313,465,504 deposits out of a total of $1,798,756,730, and yet their surplus reserve of lawful money is only about $63,600,000, or less than 5 per cent. The Southern and Western country banks, 754 in number, the 1,324 country banks of the Middle States, and the 35 banks in second class reserve cities in Bryan States, being 2,113 banks out of 3,676, hold deposits amounting to $485,291,294, and have a surplus reserve in lawful money of $55,100,000, or over 11 per cent., or nearly two and one half times the percentage of the McKinley banks. This is more clearly set forth in the following table: —

TABLE IV.

*Comparison between Eastern and Western Country Banks and Reserve Cities.*

| No. of Banks. | Class. | Deposits. | Surplus Reserve above requirements partly est'd. | Per cent. |
|---|---|---|---|---|
| 1,251 | Country banks in Eastern States . . . . . | $413,758,168 | $19,600,000 | |
| 234 | Banks in McKinley reserve cities, 2d class . | 419,561,590 | 22,000,000 | |
| 78 | Banks in reserve central . . . . . . . | 480,145,746 | 22,017,560 | |
| | | $1,313,465,504 | $63,600,000 | 4.84 |
| 754 | Country banks in Southern and Western States | $165,605,156 | $25,600,000 | |
| 1,324 | Country banks in Middle States . . . . . . | 273,725,686 | 25,500,000 | |
| 35 | Banks in Bryan reserve cities, 2d class . . . | 45,960,452 | 4,000,000 | |
| | | $485,291,294 | $55,100,000 | 11.35 |
| | Totals . . . . . | $1,798,756,798 | $118,700,000 | |

### SURPLUS RESERVES ENTIRELY TOO SMALL.

But whatever excess may be held by banks remote from financial centres is counterbalanced by the paucity in reserve carried by banks in more convenient and accessible localities, and the net result, taking the national banks as a whole, is that they had on hand, October 6, 1896, in lawful money, a surplus over the amount required by law to be held, equal to 6.6 per cent. of their demand obligations, which must be acknowledged to be entirely too small for safety.

### SURPLUS RESERVES MAY DISAPPEAR IN ONE DAY.

It is a rule among bankers that deposits seldom or never fluctuate more than 11 per cent. in one day. It is therefore evident that in the fraction of any day the banks of the country are liable to lose all their surplus lawful money reserves unless they have some other resources from which to replenish them. If the 6.6 per cent. is withdrawn by depositors, then the law requires the banks to cease discounting until their reserves are restored. This is the most prominent admonition on the blanks for quarterly reports. This means a suspension of banking facilities all over the country. It therefore becomes necessary to examine what further resources the banks have and what is their power to relieve them in case of necessity.

## EXAMINATION OF DEPOSIT RESERVES.

It is developed by this examination that the banks have credits on each other's books, a certain part of which can be called a reserve under the provisions of the National Banking Act. These deposit reserves are as shown by the following table:—

TABLE V.

*Deposit Reserves.*

| Division. | States. | No. of States. | Deposit Reserves. | Totals. | Per cent. of Deposits. |
|---|---|---|---|---|---|
| No. 7 | Col., Nev., Cal., Or. | 4 | $5,017,984 | | |
| " 4 | N. C., S. C., Ga., Fla., Ala., Miss., La., Tex., Ark., Ky., Tenn. | 11 | 10,823,072 | | |
| " 8 | S. Dak., Idaho, Mont., Utah, Wash., Wyo., N. Dak. | 7 | 5,575,697 | | |
| | Deposit reserves of banks in Southern and Western States. | | | $21,416,753 | 12.93 |
| " 5 | Ohio, Ind., Ill., Mich., Wis. | 5 | $24,131,864 | | |
| " 6 | Mo., Kan., Neb., Ia., Minn. | 5 | 12,156,785 | | |
| " 3 | Va., Del., Md., W. Va. | 4 | 5,050,329 | | |
| | Deposit reserves of banks in Middle States | | | 41,338,978 | 15.10 |
| " 2 | N. Y., N. J., Penn. | 3 | $34,851,844 | | |
| " 1 | Me., N. H., Ver., Mass., R. I., Conn. | 6 | 27,391,336 | | |
| | Deposit reserves of banks in Eastern States | | | 62,243,180 | 15.03 |
| " 1-8 | Deposit reserves of 3,329 country banks | | | $124,998,911 | |
| " 9 | Deposit reserves of 269 banks in reserve cities of second class | | | 65,078,622 | |
| | Lawful deposit reserves of all national banks. | | | $190,077,533 | |

### DEPOSIT RESERVES VALUELESS IN AN EMERGENCY.

That is, the 3,329 country banks can draw on their reserve agents for $124,990,911 in case of need, and the 269 banks in reserve cities of the second class can likewise draw on their reserve agents for $65,028,622, making a total of $190,077,533. But these reserve banks have current deposit obligations of $945,667,788, and have only a cash reserve of $224,156,056. It follows that if the country banks and banks in reserve cities of the second class should ask for their $190,000,000, there would be only $34,000,000 left to provide for the balance of the deposits of the reserve banks ($750,000,000), or about 5 per cent.

### DEMAND FOR DEPOSIT RESERVES PRODUCES SUSPENSION.

The prospect of this condition, of course, would produce a suspension for self-protection, and as a result the country banks would find at the first signal of danger that their deposit reserves were unavailable. This happened in 1893. Then came a wild scramble for currency, and every one of the 3,676 banks became, under the stimulus of the fear of receivership, a competitor with every other in an effort to hoard lawful money. The demand for money extended from the banks through all the business community, and all borrowers in the general market found their facilities withdrawn. "Liquidate and pay up" was the cry, and the result was many failures and untold losses.

Any calamity which threatens the nation is sufficient to set the ball rolling. When the reserves in the larger cities begin to decline, from whatever cause, public confidence is unsettled, and a vague feeling of apprehension takes hold of all business centres, and all financial concerns begin to fortify themselves.

#### THREAT OF RECEIVERSHIP.

It is the fundamental provision of the National Banking Act (chapter 5, section 95), that if the reserve is not made good in thirty days after notice, a receiver may be appointed for the delinquent bank. When it is considered that a loss of 6.6 per cent. of deposits would produce a simultaneous locking up of deposit reserves, and this might occur almost over night, we can see that the apprehension of business men and their solicitude over the state of the reserves is well founded.

#### STABILITY NOT POSSIBLE UNDER SUCH CONDITIONS.

Such a condition of affairs takes away all freedom from business, which must be slow and dull to be safe. If it becomes at all active and transactions are multiplied, then the feeling of confidence is liable at any moment to be interrupted by a spasm of apprehension. Stability and confidence cannot exist any length of time under such conditions.

Table V. also shows, as the previous tables have

shown, that the banks in the Southern and Western States constitute less disturbing factors than those of the Middle and Eastern States, as their percentage of deposit reserves is smaller than that of the last named States.

### ASSISTANCE FROM OTHER BANKS.

But it may be said that the report of the Comptroller shows that there are due from other national banks, besides reserve agents, $111,830,935 and from state banks, etc., 29,583,299 or a total of $141,414,234 which, added to the amount due from reserve agents, 190,077,533 makes a total for which the banks may draw on other banks, of $331,491,767

But is this a help or an aggravation? It is a help only in quiet times, but in any time of danger it is most assuredly an aggravation, because in theory the whole amount is cash, while in fact it could not be paid or collected if distrust had taken hold of the community.

A collapse in confidence must take place when one half of the reserve is found to be unavailable.

### ASSISTANCE FROM LOANS AND DISCOUNTS.

But it is urged that the banks have their bills receivable and securities to which they can have recourse for self-protection. Every business man knows what that means. It is that, if a merchant has notes out, the banks may require him to curtail or even stop his business to provide them with the funds needed to restore their reserves. Or, if a borrower has pledged securities, he may be requested to sell them at whatever sacrifice to get the cash for the bank. What more suicidal policy could be invented?

### ASSISTANCE FROM THE NEW YORK STOCK EXCHANGE.

Under such a condition of affairs a main dependence of our banks becomes the place where money can be had if it is necessary to sacrifice securities. Convertibility is the one quality demanded and relied upon. If a security is convertible it is good collateral; if it is inconvertible it is not wanted. This is a sound rule in many respects, but in others it is unsound. It leads the banks to overlook the true character of a security and rely upon a fictitious one. Legitimate business is made less desirable than speculative. Speculation is fostered and commerce is left unaided. Most borrowers have heard from bank presidents the offer of all the money they want on active stocks. During the panic of 1893 a large New York bank offered unlimited amounts to an Iowa banker if he would give stock exchange collateral. The generous offer only awakened laughter. The security held by country bankers was based on the produce of the soil, and that commanded the exchange by shipment to Europe, which brought the country safely through the pending crisis when the movement of securities was all in the contrary direction.

The banks by our system are compelled to look to the stock exchange as the most valuable adjunct to their business. When all other resources fail, when cash is gone, call loans all called in, then the stock exchange is still open, and when that shuts its doors, the clearing house also must suspend.

### CONDITION OF THE BANKS A PERIL TO THE COMMUNITY.

So the situation of our banks is that they have but a few per cent. in surplus reserves of lawful money, and when distrust has locked up their deposit reserves, their only resource to avoid a receivership is to slaughter the business community.

This diagnosis locates the disease.

# VIII

### FALLACIOUS REMEDIES

To cure the currency famine which the relative smallness of the surplus reserves renders imminent at any moment, many fallacious remedies are proposed.

#### INFLATION.

One is that the government shall issue more money, so that there shall always be an abundance. This proposition is based on ignorance and recklessness.

Those who urge an increase in the volume of government money, silver or paper, do not consider it an objection, but rather a recommendation, that such a course would surely place a premium on gold. But leaving out of the discussion the advantages or disadvantages of an irredeemable paper currency, because neither side can convince the other, it must be acknowledged that if banks are to be conducted on the credit system, which means with a reserve of only a percentage of their demand obligations on hand in cash, they are liable to calls for cash to an amount more than equal to their reserves, and at such times all floating money is in demand also. The increase of legal money does not affect the relation of a bank's demand liabilities to its reserve of lawful money. If the amount of legal money is increased beyond the needs of the country, the first effect will be that metallic money will be driven out of circulation, and the second that all commodities and services will rise in price to equal the expansion of the currency. When these two results have come to pass, the equilibrium will be restored between the amount of currency in circulation and the valuation of goods and services to be exchanged; and the relations of cash to commodities, and of reserves to liabilities, will be the same as before the suspension. The inflation will affect all equally. Then the liability to embarrassment from demands for cash in excess of reserves on hand will exist just as before the inflation. Inflation of the volume of currency cannot change the relations between reserves and demand obligations, and as a means of satisfying demands of depositors inflation is a hollow mockery. It keeps the promise to the ear and breaks it to the heart.

### CONTRACTION.

Another remedy for all ills is the cancellation of government paper, especially the greenbacks. There is a confusion of ideas in this suggestion.

The object of the retirement of the legal tenders is to relieve the government of the duty and responsibility of maintaining their payment in gold, which, however, would be no burden if the income of the government were increased so that the "endless chain" worked in the other direction. The result of retirement would be the extinguishment of a large part of the lawful money of the country. It is evident that the banks already hold too small a reserve of lawful money to admit of further diminution, and a funding of the legal tenders would be felt first by them, and a serious stringency would follow. But it is a part of the plan to have the banks either voluntarily or by compulsion subscribe for the funding bonds and use them as security for national bank circulation, so as to prevent contraction. The character of this new issue, it must be seen, would be different from the legal tenders. The currency would be changed from being the obligation of the sovereign power which only can " coin " lawful money, and made the obligation of banks, which should not be counted as part of the lawful money reserve. If it is given a forced character of lawful money, then it had better be continued as at present without placing it on an interest basis. If it is not lawful money, then it creates a vacuum in the reserves which it would be difficult for the banks to fill. If it is lawful money the condition of the banks as regards their reserve would be left just as it is at present.

The remedy does not touch the disease. It is like giving a pill to a man who has a broken leg. The difficulty with our financial situation is that we are exposed to the danger of panics because our banks have too small a reserve and have no mode for meeting additional calls without serious injury to business interests. Contraction of this kind only changes the character of a part of their reserves. It does not propose to give the banks any protection. Consequently as a remedy, the retirement of the greenbacks has no efficacy, and as a proposition to perfect our banking system it has no pertinency.

Funding the greenbacks would produce a widespread distress similar to that which was produced by the Wilson tariff. This measure of funding the greenbacks is advocated by those who believed in and secured the adoption of that tariff, and the sad experience it caused should produce in them a becoming modesty and prevent them from again urging a similar upheaval of existing conditions, lest it might be followed by a similar catastrophe.

### A MULTIPLICATION OF BANKS.

Nor is the still further multiplication of individual competitive banks a help to meet the demands of depositors or to maintain reserves and thus secure stability.

The more banks of this class there are, whether small or great, the more competitors there are for the floating cash. The battlefield is enlarged and the combatants are increased in number, but the principle of mutual destruction as the price of safety is not changed thereby. It would be a good thing to have small banks of $20,000 capital in towns of 4,000 inhabitants, provided they had access to a higher grade of banks for assistance in case of need. Without such protection, small banks had better not be created, for they would only add fuel to the flames, and many of them would be certain to meet an untimely end in their first panic. And if as large banks as the Bank of England or the Crédit Lyonnais were established, even they would need the support to be obtained. from the announcement that their bills receivable are " immediately discountable " at an issue department or a bank of a higher grade than themselves. The difference between the two banks above named is that one goes to the Bank of France without advertisement, the other with.

#### INSUFFICIENT DEVICES FOR REDEMPTION.

Another fallacious remedy is that certain devices shall be used to secure the ultimate payment of notes issued by sinking funds or a system of redemption agencies. This is based upon the idea of the children's game of " passing the ring." The one who is caught with it pays the penalty. Whoever is caught with the currency on hand at the time of the failure of the bank must wait and collect his dividends thereon as the failed bank's affairs are liquidated. This makes distrust the test of solvency, and invites runs and renders the currency of no value to perform its duty throughout the length and breadth of the land. The remedy in this case is worse than the disease. If the test question is asked, whether the banks will agree always to accept at par currency protected by these devices, the answer is promptly, No, it is only intended for the public, not for the banks.

## RELIEF BY MEANS OF A TRUSTEED CURRENCY.

As a way out of this dilemma, the proposition is made to incorporate our clearing houses under federal law, and grant to one in each State the power to receive collaterals from their bank members and advance thereon 75 per cent. in circulating notes good at any clearing house in the country, each clearing house to be the first guarantor of its own notes. This method would enable the banks to meet the wants of depositors and borrowers with a currency which would be at par all over the United States, and at the same time retain their lawful money reserves untouched. The ægis of protection should be extended over bank reserves as well as over manufactures. The approach to the apprehension minimum, and all hoarding of lawful money, and runs on banks instigated by fear of a currency famine, would be avoided.

By this system the pressure would be removed both from the banks and the business community, and monetary panics could not occur. Coöperation and not competition, peace and not strife, would be the law of banking. More conservative methods of doing business would be established and the banks could afford to carry a larger reserve of lawful money. Stability and confidence would become the permanent supports of business.

Our republican banking system can be made as preëminent among the nations of the world as is our judicial system. It needs but to be completed.

The same method by which we organize individual citizens into townships, counties, and states, and yet preserve their equality and independence, can be applied to organize individual financial interests into banks, clearing houses, and clearing house districts by bringing them all under federal control.

The elements of safety in a currency so issued are three: —

First, the actual pledge of approved security with ample margin in the hands of the state clearing house as trustee for the note-holder.

Second, the assurance the public would have of conservative action by the loan committee in judging of the goodness and adequacy of the collateral pledged, from their experience and ability, their representative position, and their pecuniary interest as stockholders in banks which they would endeavor to protect from loss on their contingent liability as guarantors.

Third, the guarantee by the associated banks to save the note-holder from loss or delay in the payment of the notes.

Fourth, protection of legal reserves and consequent monetary stability.

These characteristics are general and should be effective under all circumstances, in any State or Territory, to produce conservative action and to give a safe currency to the whole nation.

# IX

## A DISCUSSION OF PRACTICAL DIFFICULTIES IN THE WAY OF A UNIVERSAL SYSTEM

### IS DIFFERENCE IN ACCUMULATED WEALTH AN OBJECTION TO A UNIVERSAL SYSTEM?

It may be objected that the loans and currency issued in one part of the United States would not be so safe as those issued in another, and that the banks in the richer States could not afford to agree to take at par and hold, even for the short time needed to forward them for collection, the notes issued and secured in what have been styled the poorer States.

This presents a question which must be solved, and a comparison must be made between the different sections of our land to discover what foundation there is for this objection.

We have already seen that the Southern and Western States hold the largest percentage in lawful money.

The basis of the present comparison must be the ratio of debts to assets in each section. The convenient mode of comparison used in Table I. (see p. 50), is here followed again. The States are divided into two classes, those which gave their electoral votes to McKinley and those which gave them to Bryan in the last presidential election. This has the advantage in that it separates what have been called the rich and the poor States, and thus takes an extreme view of the situation. The following tables have been prepared, in pursuance of this method, from figures published by the Comptroller of the Currency and the Secretary of Agriculture. They were used in a similar manner in a presentation of this subject before Congress.

An examination of these tables will show that there is no ground for the objection that there is in the varying financial conditions of the different sections of the country an insuperable obstacle to the adoption of a system intended to apply alike to all sections.

At a glance it will appear from these tables that the Bryan States have the largest area and room for future growth. Nine of these, with 4,000,000 inhabitants, have sprung into being in fifty years. The new States are now growing more rapidly than the old. Comparing banking conditions, bank deposits in the Bryan States are hardly twice the banking capital of those States, while in McKinley States they are two and one half times.

## TABLE VI.

*Financial Statistics of all States.*

| STATES. | Area. | Population. | No. of Banks. | Capital Stock. | Individual Deposits. | Loans and Discounts. | Stocks and Securities. | Personal Property. | Real Property. | Farm Lands. | Farm Products. | Manufactured Products. | Real Estate Mortgages. |
|---|---|---|---|---|---|---|---|---|---|---|---|---|---|
| 1 | 2 | 3 | 4 | 5 | 6 | 7 | 8 | 9 | 10 | 11 | 12 | 13 | 14 |
| *McKinley States.* | *Sq. m.* | | | $ | $ | $ | $ | $ | $ | $ | $ | $ | $ |
| Maine | 29,895 | 661,086 | 82 | 11,156,000 | 15,629,057 | 22,619,626 | 2,255,886 | 253,064,569 | 254,069,589 | 98,505,770 | 22,049,220 | 93,480,500 | 22,627,208 |
| New Hampshire | 9,005 | 376,530 | 50 | 5,630,000 | 8,624,732 | 10,260,455 | 2,768,477 | 148,867,740 | 176,131,000 | 65,102,030 | 15,761,050 | 85,770,549 | 18,968,520 |
| Vermont | 9,135 | 332,422 | 49 | 6,258,000 | 8,542,300 | 12,150,195 | 1,670,129 | 127,180,929 | 158,057,734 | 80,457,490 | 20,364,560 | 28,340,032 | 25,307,086 |
| Massachusetts | 8,040 | 2,238,943 | 268 | 95,277,300 | 161,847,137 | 244,741,615 | 16,253,076 | 365,007,655 | 1,898,657,734 | 127,678,584 | 29,072,500 | 888,160,403 | 35,277,028 |
| Rhode Island | 1,085 | 345,506 | 82 | 19,317,050 | 13,077,574 | 35,022,729 | 3,022,352 | 123,422,510 | 334,240,002 | 21,873,479 | 4,218,800 | 132,500,055 | 31,778,343 |
| Connecticut | 4,845 | 746,258 | 97 | 22,291,070 | 32,455,361 | 45,497,618 | 7,120,708 | 291,686,328 | 543,421,801 | 35,000,805 | 17,924,310 | 248,336,264 | 70,921,671 |
| New York | 47,620 | 5,997,853 | 527 | 85,486,040 | 383,903,438 | 425,984,186 | 22,227,553 | 2,774,807,324 | 5,817,704,067 | 368,127,206 | 161,505,020 | 1,711,577,657 | 1,097,074,301 |
| New Jersey | 7,455 | 1,414,933 | 162 | 14,383,000 | 32,123,193 | 51,428,414 | 8,348,248 | 484,571,142 | 961,401,072 | 132,292,440 | 28,107,340 | 354,573,767 | 232,745,910 |
| Pennsylvania | 44,985 | 5,258,014 | 419 | 74,065,820 | 152,143,550 | 242,863,584 | 32,383,782 | 2,409,363,263 | 3,781,177,585 | 322,240,235 | 121,729,348 | 1,311,794,301 | 613,105,802 |
| Delaware | 1,960 | 168,493 | 18 | 2,155,585 | 4,784,875 | 5,299,701 | 468,611 | 69,208,270 | 103,729,519 | 39,585,000 | 6,461,200 | 25,571,185 | 16,122,086 |
| Maryland | 9,860 | 1,042,390 | 68 | 17,054,800 | 23,110,305 | 41,524,582 | 3,460,422 | 240,165,181 | 473,058,570 | 173,058,550 | 26,443,761 | 171,842,593 | 64,577,883 |
| West Virginia | 24,645 | 762,794 | 78 | 3,411,040 | 7,100,781 | 8,945,921 | 460,485 | 100,227,404 | 248,727,477 | 151,480,300 | 20,479,000 | 36,571,148 | 19,702,505 |
| Ohio | 40,760 | 3,672,316 | 251 | 45,370,100 | 92,019,431 | 106,110,949 | 9,106,795 | 1,421,127,302 | 1,288,162,242 | 1,094,053,828 | 133,222,499 | 229,825,082 | 259,842,188 |
| Indiana | 35,910 | 2,012,880 | 113 | 14,202,000 | 23,674,637 | 31,388,570 | 2,704,000 | 707,012,880 | 1,172,769,279 | 754,789,110 | 94,759,292 | 169,460,290 | 184,259,150 |
| Illinois | 56,000 | 3,826,351 | 221 | 39,221,000 | 162,544,236 | 125,476,844 | 2,574,020 | 843,225,818 | 1,288,165,271 | 1,262,870,597 | 184,789,015 | 277,686,706 | 110,720,045 |
| Michigan | 57,430 | 2,093,889 | 91 | 13,192,000 | 24,868,155 | 42,548,365 | 10,118,562 | 343,225,818 | 1,234,612,440 | 556,190,020 | 85,651,290 | 248,546,161 | 150,472,700 |
| Wisconsin | 54,450 | 1,686,880 | 81 | 10,445,000 | 22,514,321 | 22,498,075 | 1,464,878 | 742,957,832 | 1,108,251,201 | 477,524,505 | 70,810,643 | 192,025,478 | 121,826,148 |
| Minnesota | 83,365 | 1,301,825 | 166 | 14,830,000 | 31,184,722 | 36,462,155 | 1,712,680 | 637,689,772 | 1,131,162,155 | 340,059,470 | 71,259,270 | 125,049,103 | 196,745,989 |
| Iowa | 55,475 | 1,911,896 | 259 | 13,085,000 | 33,235,111 | 36,831,727 | 2,254,032 | 1,025,647,725 | 1,561,701,010 | 825,861,122 | 159,347,884 | 35,129,107 | 199,774,171 |
| North Dakota | 70,195 | 182,719 | 29 | 1,810,000 | 5,047,945 | 4,362,140 | 384,846 | 163,083,407 | 469,458,928 | 73,390,203 | 21,304,488 | 136,719,857 | 25,177,180 |
| Kentucky | 40,000 | 1,858,635 | 77 | 13,084,400 | 13,640,255 | 26,075,833 | 1,060,014 | 401,221,391 | 715,293,088 | 346,330,307 | 65,396,485 | 41,462,174 | 45,650,740 |
| Oregon | 94,560 | 313,767 | 53 | 3,170,000 | 7,347,681 | 6,372,278 | 1,117,570 | 230,174,803 | 591,174,803 | 113,819,300 | 19,054,120 | 213,465,896 | 22,928,437 |
| California | 155,980 | 1,208,130 | 31 | 9,225,000 | 16,161,285 | 16,574,365 | 1,174,388 | 802,619,572 | 1,071,113,635 | 637,116,630 | 87,055,240 | | 241,050,184 |
| Total | 938,495 | 34,624,035 | 2,735 | 524,162,625 | 1,230,151,382 | 1,615,859,174 | 165,655,911 | 17,160,807,388 | 25,558,955,024 | 9,459,580,156 | 1,462,124,725 | 4,152,125,207 | 4,822,882,018 |

## FINANCIAL STATISTICS

75

| 1 | 2 | 3 | 4 | 5 | 6 | 7 | 8 | 9 | 10 | 11 | 12 | 13 | 14 |
|---|---|---|---|---|---|---|---|---|---|---|---|---|---|
| *Bryan States.* | | | | | | | | | | | | | |
| Virginia | 40,125 | 1,665,990 | 37 | 4,796,300 | 13,591,874 | 15,261,317 | 1,157,518 | 391,675,517 | 470,649,555 | 254,490,000 | 42,244,458 | 88,363,624 | 28,691,726 |
| North Carolina | 48,540 | 1,617,917 | 28 | 2,766,000 | 4,823,868 | 6,452,705 | 316,900 | 305,173,773 | 278,575,226 | 183,967,010 | 50,070,500 | 40,575,450 | 21,471,428 |
| South Carolina | 30,170 | 1,151,149 | 15 | 1,848,000 | 2,744,483 | 5,886,244 | 931,436 | 224,382,851 | 176,528,352 | 19,104,000 | 51,357,485 | 31,926,681 | 13,780,312 |
| Georgia | 58,940 | 1,857,733 | 28 | 4,016,000 | 6,654,482 | 8,525,936 | 822,814 | 217,070,065 | 415,239,584 | 152,000,820 | 82,371,482 | 68,997,629 | 27,385,580 |
| Florida | 54,240 | 391,422 | 17 | 1,359,800 | 5,911,451 | 3,567,424 | 744,427 | 183,871,880 | 185,614,258 | 72,745,340 | 12,686,270 | 18,222,850 | 15,506,119 |
| Missouri | 68,735 | 2,670,184 | 65 | 16,613,400 | 22,239,542 | 45,174,149 | 7,044,468 | 939,171,744 | 1,438,733,201 | 623,858,293 | 109,751,024 | 224,591,993 | 214,005,772 |
| South Dakota | 76,850 | 324,898 | 30 | 1,885,000 | 3,069,700 | 3,148,504 | 621,174 | 218,218,098 | 203,825,291 | 107,460,235 | 22,047,279 | 5,682,746 | 26,115,773 |
| Nebraska | 76,840 | 1,628,910 | 112 | 10,975,400 | 17,057,122 | 19,302,617 | 1,295,022 | 507,272,416 | 708,413,098 | 402,258,513 | 68,957,017 | 103,037,794 | 122,902,222 |
| Kansas | 81,700 | 1,427,096 | 116 | 9,552,100 | 15,245,125 | 17,408,248 | 944,888 | 658,812,325 | 929,580,178 | 559,725,044 | 55,070,084 | 110,219,805 | 243,146,895 |
| Tennessee | 41,750 | 1,767,518 | 45 | 6,277,400 | 13,325,020 | 18,179,988 | 957,029 | 404,104,035 | 485,703,510 | 242,706,540 | 55,194,104 | 72,335,285 | 40,423,286 |
| Alabama | 51,540 | 1,513,017 | 27 | 3,405,000 | 5,727,707 | 6,417,525 | 1,152,455 | 323,493,560 | 271,963,944 | 111,063,380 | 66,240,100 | 51,226,063 | 22,025,388 |
| Mississippi | 46,340 | 1,289,600 | 30 | 855,000 | 2,022,424 | 2,054,225 | 414,322 | 245,840,064 | 208,283,024 | 125,423,117 | 73,842,365 | 18,702,684 | 19,075,180 |
| Louisiana | 45,420 | 1,118,887 | 18 | 2,893,000 | 14,081,010 | 12,882,970 | 2,229,325 | 283,528,731 | 271,961,946 | 83,381,270 | 54,343,833 | 57,806,713 | 28,313,949 |
| Texas | 262,290 | 2,235,723 | 207 | 20,921,000 | 20,532,776 | 28,938,008 | 1,782,947 | 885,178,968 | 1,229,417,771 | 308,937,289 | 111,689,430 | 70,455,577 | 163,864,178 |
| Arkansas | 53,045 | 392,179 | 25 | 1,239,100 | 4,603,422 | 3,255,452 | 117,671 | 221,289,291 | 253,855,133 | 118,574,422 | 83,128,135 | 22,650,170 | 14,736,595 |
| Wyoming | 97,575 | 122,130 | 11 | 389,000 | 1,418,179 | 3,610,487 | 1,231,128 | 243,324,412 | 207,770,707 | 5,312,540 | 6,275,415 | 5,367,527 | 8,729,401 |
| Montana | 162,645 | 412,198 | 42 | 5,487,000 | 11,455,721 | 7,721,865 | 917,361 | 77,280,330 | 92,493,557 | 14,404,880 | 2,241,500 | 2,357,701 | 4,942,065 |
| Colorado | 82,190 | 207,905 | 11 | 1,889,000 | 24,280,410 | 18,001,653 | 1,225,550 | 549,391,102 | 603,296,165 | 85,625,140 | 13,126,910 | 42,480,395 | 85,058,758 |
| Utah | 101,740 | 45,761 | 11 | 82,000 | 2,584,555 | 2,690,657 | 272,888 | 165,368,381 | 183,117,232 | 28,482,740 | 4,801,020 | 4,911,047 | 8,040,929 |
| Nevada | 84,280 | 84,385 | 11 | 575,000 | 181,412 | 151,412 | 9,546 | 88,100,683 | 192,222,975 | 12,329,410 | 2,703,050 | 1,105,079 | 2,194,495 |
| Idaho | 66,880 | 318,230 | 40 | 4,778,000 | 1,840,374 | 1,197,773 | 517,488 | 112,283,744 | 95,900,907 | 17,451,540 | 3,948,830 | 1,386,088 | 3,167,249 |
| Washington | | | | | 4,438,497 | 7,658,012 | 1,146,172 | 244,523,577 | 516,365,149 | 83,461,607 | 12,675,059 | 41,768,022 | 44,058,449 |
| Total | 1,726,255 | 22,412,776 | 909 | 108,370,400 | 214,123,242 | 246,462,715 | 25,157,276 | 7,965,946,575 | 9,311,533,418 | 3,608,474,173 | 985,588,484 | 1,178,030,980 | 1,125,110,186 |
| Total of States | 2,054,730 | 62,116,811 | 3,044 | 624,683,325 | 1,466,274,684 | 1,462,242,089 | 104,732,887 | 25,151,737,968 | 26,501,349,042 | 12,248,877,329 | 2,456,463,919 | 3,199,350,154 | 5,358,700,204 |

The figures contained in these tables are condensed in the following table, which makes a comparison between loans and discounts, real and personal property, farm products, manufactures, and mortgages of the McKinley and Bryan States.

### TABLE VII.
*Percentage of Assets to Obligations.*

|  | Loans and Discounts. | Real and Personal Property. | Loans and Discounts, Percentage of. |
|---|---|---|---|
| Bryan States | $246,482,715 | $17,275,299,993 | 1.42 |
| McKinley States | 1,615,859,374 | 46,789,803,012 | 3.45 |
| United States | 1,862,342,089 | 64,065,103,005 | 2.91 |

|  | Farm Products. | Loans and Discounts, Percentage of. | Manufactures. | Loans and Discounts, Percentage of. |
|---|---|---|---|---|
| Bryan States | $993,538,484 | 24.70 | $1,178,030,080 | 20.92 |
| McKinley States | 1,462,924,735 | 110.45 | 8,152,123,307 | 19.82 |
| United States | 2,456,463,219 | 75.81 | 9,330,154,287 | 19.95 |

|  | Mortgages. | Real Estate. | Proportion of Mortgages to Real Estate. |
|---|---|---|---|
| Bryan States | $1,125,118,186 | $9,311,353,418 | 12.08 |
| McKinley States | 4,833,582,018 | 29,590,995,624 | 16.36 |
| United States | 5,958,700,204 | 38,911,349,042 | 15.31 |

This is a comparison between debts and assets, which every merchant knows affords the only true basis.

## COMPARISON OF LOANS AND DISCOUNTS.

It appears that the loans and discounts of the McKinley States are 3.45 per cent. of the real and personal property of those States, while in the Bryan States the percentage is only 1.42 per cent. That is, the percentage of banking debts to assets is over twice as great in the McKinley States as in the Bryan States.

## COMPARISON OF FARM PRODUCTS.

The comparison as regards farm products is still more striking. The loans and discounts of the Bryan States are but 24.70 per cent. of the annual farm products of those States. That is, the farm products could pay all their banking discounts four times over in one year. In the McKinley States the annual farm products fall short by 10.45 per cent. of the banking discounts of those States. In panic years this enormous surplus in the Bryan States has not only helped them, but the whole country, by supplying exports which commanded the cash when the best securities were unavailable.

## COMPARISON OF MANUFACTURED PRODUCTS.

The percentage of manufactured products to their respective bank discounts is nearly the same in the two sections, and requires no comment, except to call attention to the fact, which to many may be a surprise, that the difference is only a little under one per cent.

## COMPARISON OF BURDEN OF MORTGAGES.

In comparing the burden of mortgages to the value of real estate, again the showing is in favor of the Bryan States, their proportion of indebtedness being only 12.08 per cent., while that of the McKinley States is 16.36 per cent.

## ALL COMPARISONS FAVORABLE TO BRYAN STATES.

Thus it appears that in all comparisons between liabilities and assets, the statistics show that the Bryan States have greater room for growth and a more promising future for development, a larger proportion of bank capital to deposits, a greater surplus of farm products, are carrying a lighter burden of fixed charges in comparison with their annual products, have more recuperative power, and have a greater value of real estate to their mortgages than the McKinley States.

## ADVANTAGES AND DISADVANTAGES OF DIFFERENT SECTIONS COMPARED.

The key to any comparison between different sections of the country must be found in the proportion of resources to obligations. It cannot be denied, however, that it is safer to lend 75 per cent. on a convertible asset, than 35 per cent. on an inconvertible one, the intrinsic value being the same. This explains the difference between the situation in the East and in the West and South. The severe experience of the past few years has contracted banking facilities and deprived Western and Southern communities of the ability to trade, and thereby made inconvertible much property which formerly had a ready market, and made business unsafe which once paid a regular profit.

Any banking system worthy to be adopted by Congress must be applicable to all parts of the country alike, and it is evident from the figures given in tables I. to VII. that one section cannot claim a superiority over another either in prudent management or in abundant resources.

No rule can be made which will apply to irregular and speculative banking. All loans and discounts must be judged by their individual merits. Surprises will happen in every section of the country. But a generalization can be made on the prominent facts made apparent by statistics. It must be allowed that banking can be conducted safely in a country where the farm products will pay the total of bank discounts four times over each year, and yet all banking there is not necessarily safe. It is also apparent that a system of banking which relies on forced liquidations as a means of maintaining bank reserves operates with special hardship and severity on communities which have not ready access to exchanges and central markets, and whose assets, though solid, are not convertible. Such communities become prostrated, so that they may not recover the lost ground in a generation, while a system which would carry them over panics, and avoid liquidations, would prevent untold disasters and favor their rapid growth.

One section of the country is not independent of another; but the cotton, breadstuffs, and provisions of the Southern and Western States afford the country the largest items with which its foreign debts are paid. As these command the cash in the markets of the world, so they afford the best basis for credit at home.

### CASH VALUATIONS UNIVERSAL.

In any banking system all commodities are reduced to their cash value, and money thus becomes a common denominator the world over. Cotton may be raised in a section poor in accumulated capital, but it commands the gold in Liverpool as well as New York. Wheat likewise may come from the inhospitable North, but it grades and sells equally well in all corn exchanges of every nation. Cattle are raised on plains not adapted for farming, but their product fills solid trains from the West to the East. All these products form as good a basis for banking as the garden truck of populous counties near our great cities, unless some as yet undiscovered law of finance be found to prove that a dollar's worth of produce from one locality is worth more than a dollar's worth produced in another. Commodities which can be turned into cash in the open market have no superiority the one over the other. Money is as clean when made in packing hogs as in manufacturing silk, and one business is as necessary and as honorable as the other. The strength of a bank does not depend upon the wealth of the community in which it does business, but on the character of the assets it holds. A bank in Hongkong or Shanghai, China, may have the highest commercial rating, and this would rest on the fact that its assets are known to be convertible into cash at the prices given in the balance sheet. Money is the common denominator in which all commodities are exchanged, and the ores of Colorado and Alabama and Michigan form equally good banking security at proportionate values when moving to market, whether in crude form or as finished products. The American dollar goes from one end of our country to the other, measuring the values of commodities, and it is the great leveler to bring all things to a common standard. Wheat, corn, cotton, lumber, tobacco, and cattle are not inferior to any other commodities, and they form a solid basis for credit to their producers.

A thousand dollars' worth of cotton, wheat, or tobacco will all pay the same amount of debts in New York without regard to the populousness or wealth of the sections from which they have come. All banking is ultimately founded on products of the soil, the mines, and the factory, and the question to ask is, not as to the accumulated advantages of one section over another, but how the sections can be compared in ability to pay their debts, and what is the cash value of the products.

The following statement of the banking situation in seven Southern States brings this contrast strikingly into view.

## TABLE VIII.

*Seven Southern States.*

| State. | Number of Banks. | Capital Stock. | Deposits. | Loans and Discounts. | Farm Products. |
|---|---|---|---|---|---|
| North Carolina | 28 | $2,766,000 | $4,869,968 | $6,432,705 | $50,070,530 |
| South Carolina | 15 | 1,848,000 | 3,744,481 | 5,856,344 | 51,337,985 |
| Georgia | 28 | 4,016,000 | 6,634,493 | 8,925,609 | 83,371,482 |
| Florida | 17 | 1,350,000 | 3,911,651 | 3,567,624 | 12,086,330 |
| Alabama | 27 | 3,405,000 | 5,727,797 | 6,417,525 | 66,240,190 |
| Mississippi | 10 | 855,000 | 2,032,424 | 2,034,329 | 73,342,995 |
| Arkansas | 9 | 1,220,000 | 1,661,422 | 2,355,437 | 53,128,155 |
| Total | 134 | 15,460,000 | 28,582,236 | 35,589,573 | 380,577,667 |
| Average | 19 | 2,208,571 | 4,083,176 | 5,084,224 | 55,653,952 |

This table shows that business in these seven States must be much restricted for want of banking facilities, and could be enlarged with entire safety.

### ANNUAL FARM PRODUCTS TEN TIMES BANK DISCOUNTS.

That the legitimate loans and discounts in these seven States are well secured admits of little question when it is seen that the average farm products are each year ten times the total amount of the loans and discounts made by the national banks in those States. Paper that is issued to bring cotton to market is as good as any other kind. It would form the best basis for local issues of currency when pledged with a state clearing house as trustee for the public. It would be imposing no onerous condition on the banks of the country to oblige them to accept currency so secured at any clearing house in the land, and every banker would know that losses to the banks on such currency would be well-nigh impossible.

The security which would be offered at clearing house would be the choice of all the best assets of each applying bank. The currency issued would therefore be based on the best business obligations of the country.

If, however, the banks in these States were allowed to issue currency on their own judgment, in their own back parlors, without supervision, and hold the security themselves, the way would be opened for a repetition of the disasters of 1837 which were produced by that style of banking.

### HOW WOULD THE SYSTEM WORK IN A BAD YEAR?

We know from experience what the results have been of the present national banking system during the good and bad years since its inauguration. We know the results of banking under the competitive system of individual bank liability for an unsecured circulation which prevailed in this country in 1837. We know also the results of the systems which have prevailed in France, Germany, and England during the past twenty-five years. But it may be claimed that our country presents special difficulties for the establishment of any new system, and it is right to inquire how the system of incorporated clearing houses with special powers to issue a clearing house circulation would have operated during some of the bad years we have lately experienced. It may be well to endeavor to answer this question, and, for an example, take the year 1893, and endeavor to analyze the national bank failures of that year.

### BAD YEARS WOULD BE LESS FREQUENT.

First it must be evident that with a system of incorporated clearing houses, and a reserve of $600,000,000, or the par of the total banking capital of the nation, the panic of 1893 could not have swept the country as it did. There is no mystery about that panic, for it was simply the operation of competitive banking with a small reserve. Banks and individuals all over the country began to strengthen themselves by accumulating a larger supply of gold and legal tenders when they saw the reserves diminishing. As the supply vanished the demand grew stronger for the restoration of reserves, and it only abated when enough good business had been closed out and destroyed to pile up a large supply of idle currency in the banks. Such a panic strikes the country like a squall, and there is no time to make new provision; reliance can only be had on past accumulations.

### BANK FAILURES IN 1893.

The Comptroller of the Currency reports 69 national banks for which receivers were appointed during the year 1893 in 25 States and 1 Territory.

Of the 25 States, 14 were Bryan with 46 banks, 11 McKinley with 22 banks. Of the 46 banks, 9 were restored to solvency, and of the 22, 2, leaving 37 Bryan banks and 20 McKinley.

OUTCOME OF SUSPENDED BANKS.

Of the 69 suspended banks, in addition to the 11 which were restored to solvency without administration by the receiver, there were 6 which paid in full without assessment on the stockholders. Three more paid in full with only a small stock assessment. Here are 20 banks, almost one third of the failures whose subsequent history proves that if a system had then been in operation by which they could have had temporary assistance, they would not have been obliged to fail. While we are seeking to encourage the establishment of new banks, is it not a better policy to save and protect those we have? There is a second class of these banks, 13 in number, which have paid dividends from 60 to 100 per cent., and have assets remaining which in some cases may yield enough to pay out nearly, if not quite in full.

There are 36 banks more which have paid only from 10 to 60 per cent. with not much promise for the future, though the nominal assets in some instances are large.

The 69 failed national banks of 1893 may be listed thus: —

## TABLE IX.
*Suspended National Banks of* 1893.

11 banks restored to solvency,
6   "     paid in full without assessment.
3   "    "   "   "   with slight   "
---
20 banks which needed slight assistance.

2 banks which have paid 90 to 100%.
4   "    "    "    "   80 to 90%.
3   "    "    "    "   70 to 80%.
4   "    "    "    "   60 to 70%.
---
13 banks with considerable remaining assets.

15 banks which have paid 50 to 60%.
3   "    "    "    "   40 to 50%.
8   "    "    "    "   30 to 40%.
5   "    "    "    "   20 to 30 .
5   "    "    "    "   10 to 20 .
---
36 banks without much future prospects.
---
69 total number of national banks failed in 1893.

The record of the national banks for 1893 is no doubt about the same as we would find to be true as regards state banks and trust companies, and many private firms; that is, that slight additional assistance at the critical point would have stayed the ravages of the panic and saved the country untold losses, and probably prevented one half or more of the failures.

### LOANS TO SOME OF THESE BANKS COULD HAVE BEEN MADE SAFELY.

The remaining question is whether this could have been done with entire safety to those advancing the credit.

This question must be answered in the affirmative if the advances had been made by experienced bankers, acquainted with the concerns applying for aid and with the collateral security they offered, and who themselves were interested in avoiding a loss on the advances. If a loan committee is to pass upon the sufficiency of the collateral, and the members of that committee are stockholders in banks connected with the clearing house for which they are acting, and their banks have a proportionate liability for any loss which may result from such loans, it may be safely assumed that they will see to it that the security is good and ample, and losses may be as rare as they have been on clearing house certificates. Members of a bank committee are specially trained for that work. The effect of this supervision would be most salutary on the banks, for in order to be able to obtain advances from the clearing house, their notes and collateral securities must be of a high class. Many a bank would be restrained from taking certain low grades of paper if it was known they would not pass at the clearing house. The whole fabric of banking assets would be improved, and the entire method of banking would be made more conservative, as it has been in France, by the supervision which would thus be established in the clearing houses.

That advances to these 69 banks which failed in 1893 could have been made safely is shown by the amount of cash collected from their assets.

## TABLE X.
### Cash Collections of Suspended Banks.

| | |
|---|---:|
| The total capital of these 69 banks was | $11,520,000 |
| Deduct capital of 11 banks restored to solvency | 1,725,000 |
| Total capital of banks administered by receivers | 9,795,000 |
| There has been collected in cash from the assets of these banks. | 11,087,491 |
| And there are remaining in hands of receivers nominal assets amounting to about | 13,000,000 |

This statement shows that if ordinary prudence had been exercised, loans to these failed banks on their assets would not have resulted in loss to those who might have advanced them credit to an amount not more than their capital stock.

Under the German system it must be especially noticed that the privilege to issue an emergency currency is only conferred on a few large banks. It would be dangerous in the extreme to confer it in our country on small clearing houses generally. There must be some combination of banks to produce the responsibility which can be compared with that of the Imperial Bank. This it is proposed to accomplish by conferring the control of currency issues upon one clearing house in each State or on any making clearings of over $200,000,000 annually.

## REDEMPTION.

The burden of the redemption of the currency is placed upon the clearing houses. If the public should desire to collect any of these notes, they need only to deposit them in any bank, and the cash would stand at their credit. If the notes should accumulate at any centre, the banks would sort and collect them as any other drafts. The public would not be interested in the arrangement which banks and clearing houses might make between themselves for such collections. The mode of collection through any clearing house is summary. Payment of the notes on demand is indispensable to restrain the issues and keep them always on a cash basis.

### ELASTICITY.

It is sometimes said that elasticity cannot be attained with a secured currency. A currency may be secured by pledge with a trustee of either bonds or bank assets. The national bank currency is a type of one class, and New York clearing house certificates are a type of the other.

### CAN ELASTICITY BE ATTAINED WITH A SECURED CURRENCY?

The general statement that elasticity cannot be attained with a secured currency is based upon an experience with a bond-security purchased for the sake of taking out currency, and it is true as far as it applies to that. Lack of elasticity in a bond-secured currency has been noticed ever since the enactment of the New York free banking law of 1838. Inelasticity was the cause of the first issue of clearing house certificates in 1857, which were elastic because secured by bank assets. When the National Currency Act was passed in 1863, the chief criticism then was that currency so issued must be inelastic. The criticism is as old as a bond-secured currency, has never been denied, and must be accepted as true.

### CURRENCY ELASTIC WHEN SECURED BY BANK ASSETS.

But it is not true of a currency issued on pledge of the assets of a bank, its bills receivable, and other securities taken in the ordinary course of commercial business. An issue of currency secured by these assets would be put out to meet the demands of depositors, or to furnish discounts in excess of the loanable funds of the bank. If the funds of the bank are first loaned to regular customers, and thereafter, when money becomes active, the assets thus accumulated are pledged to secure currency, then the funds of the bank are released to be loaned again. When the demand is over, and deposits return, and the discounts are paid, then the bank would return its currency and take up its collateral. This expansion and contraction is called elasticity, and it can as well be obtained under a trusteeship as if the banks should issue the currency and hold the security themselves.

### DIFFERENCE BETWEEN BOND AND ASSET SECURITY.

The nature of the two transactions involved in the issue of currency on bonds on the one hand, or on bank assets on the other, is different. The first is an investment of a margin of money in the purchase of bonds, to be lodged as security for currency, for the sake of the profit in the operation. The transaction is one more loan or investment of the funds of the bank. The investment in the margin pays a certain profit, and if that profit is above the rate of interest at which money can be loaned by the bank, the bank will take out currency liberally. If it is below that rate, then the bank will take out only the minimum amount required by law.

If a bank has taken out currency on an easy money market, and rates afterwards advance so that taking currency becomes less profitable than loaning the margin, then if the bank can sell its deposited bonds without loss, it would be inclined to do so. With the proceeds it would retire its currency, and lend to its customers the margin thus released. So we should have the paradoxical state of affairs under a system of currency secured by bonds, that banks might retire their currency on a close money market in order to increase their loanable funds. This is creating more money by contracting the amount in circulation. This contraction would take place when the banks could accommodate their customers better and make more profit to themselves by lending the capital direct, instead of using it as margin on a purchase of bonds.

## CURRENCY SECURED BY BONDS OF LITTLE SERVICE.

There is a difficulty which is almost insurmountable in making of any service to the commercial community a currency which is obtained on bonds. This lack of elasticity has been commented on in every panic since 1857. In the worst of the panic of 1893 the benefit derived from national bank currency was almost nothing.[1] This is because the owners of United States bonds are not the class in need of assistance, and even in a period of extreme stringency arrangements can hardly be made by commercial banks to obtain bonds to be pledged for currency and at the same time retain the currency for the benefit of their commercial customers. Currency obtained on bonds has nothing to do with the commercial business of the bank, which is rigidly confined to its actual loanable cash.

The two transactions show that a secured currency may be either elastic or rigid. A bond-security necessarily produces an inelastic currency, and bank assets produce an elastic currency, whether held by the bank or pledged with a trustee. So it must be allowed that elasticity can be attained with a currency secured by property in the hands of a trustee, provided the property is convertible bank assets. The elasticity is due to the difference in the security and not to the difference in its custodian.

[1] On this point, see Appendix, p. 226.

## BANKS CANNOT UNITE ON A PLAN FOR A NEW SYSTEM.

While there exists a widespread desire for a reformation of our financial system, it is a remarkable fact that banks as a class have no measure which they are united in advocating. They attempted to formulate such a measure when they prepared what is known as the Baltimore plan, but when that was put into shape, the banks almost unanimously abandoned it. It would be supposed at first sight that the officers of banks, who have a daily experience in bank management, would be especially acquainted with the defects of the existing system, and would be well qualified to suggest remedies.

One reason for their failure to do so is that in the ordinary daily routine the existing system works well. Business can be conducted under it with satisfaction to the stockholders and customers. Panics arise from difficulties with which a local bank has nothing to do; they belong to a range of questions that lie beyond its daily routine, and the local officer feels he is not in a position to grasp and systematize the factors of the problem. He therefore contentedly settles down to his work and leaves the whole subject to others who are, he thinks, in a better position than he to deal with it.

Another reason is that he says in effect, Prepare your new system, and if I like it I will conform to it; if not, I have the option of retiring from the business. This is a reasonable position, and perhaps is the one most commonly taken. The officers of to-day had no voice in the formation of the present system, and are now working under it only as a way of making money. They are interested parties, and the suggestions of changes they might make would only be in the direction of making the system more profitable to the banks, not more serviceable to the public. Their chief object is not to prevent panics and save the commercial community from losses, but to take care of their own interests, assuming that the parties of the second part will take care of their side of the bargain. They therefore see the propriety of referring to Congress the reconstruction of the system, and they content themselves with their power of choice if any new provisions are deemed onerous.

Another reason for failure is the diversity of political opinions among bankers which prevents them from union upon a plan. The great division is into Republicans and Democrats, — the one sustaining a national system, under a general federal law; the other preferring a state system, under special charters. It has been said that it is as incorrect to speak of Republican and Democratic money as of Republican or Democratic potatoes. Political history, however, shows that such a difference exists. The whole current of Republican legislation on banking has led up to and ends in the national banking system, with its general laws, governmental supervision, statistical reports, and security for circulation in the hands of a trustee, that is, government bonds pledged with the treasurer of the United States in trust. This is a development of banking which is one of the greatest glories of republican institutions, the like of which is not seen in any other country. Democratic legislation has ended in the state system, with special charters, and no trusteeship for the currency. There is, therefore, a radical difference between Republican and Democratic money, and bank officers belonging to these parties cannot unite upon a common plan.

Another division of bankers is formed by those who have received their education in other countries, or who are enamored of English and other precedents, and who advocate foreign systems as the only true sources of relief. They can hardly conceal their contempt for American banking, and suggest systems of branch banks dominated by a parent institution with overshadowing capital, or the revival of the Bank of the United States in some form. The supporters of these plans ignore our political divisions into separate States, and sometimes traduce the memory of Andrew Jackson for having overthrown the United States Bank, the only effect of which is to place themselves outside of the discussion. These many political differences necessarily prevent united action on the part of banks.

#### CHANGES MUST BE MADE BY CONGRESS.

The changes in our system must be made by Congress, which holds the constitutional power to pass laws regulating the currency. In Congress is the arena where all parties, all financial interests, and all theories can meet in open discussion, and there the question must be decided.

Banking must be brought to conform to our political system. It is not only a matter of business. Congress occupies the position of arbitrator between the banks and the business community, both of which parties are to receive full consideration and neither of them to be ignored. But above all, fidelity to the principles on which our government is established must be jealously maintained.

### CONCLUSION.

We have now finished the attempt to present the argument in support of the position that a system of clearing houses incorporated under federal law, with power to issue currency on pledge of collateral by their members, would protect the commercial community from panic and provide whatever money is needed for legitimate business. This is all that the commercial community want of a banking system. It can also be claimed that under the supervision of loan committees, the chance of loss to the banks of the remaining States, resulting from injudicious loans sufficient to extinguish all the banking capital of a single State, would be small enough to be ignored. The practical result would no doubt be that very little clearing house currency would be issued, and that hereafter banking would be conducted with little disturbance, and interest charges would be more regular and uniform. The banks would keep in reserve the power to issue clearing house currency, and that reserve would maintain tranquillity, and support and protect commercial credit.

It has come to be an axiom among bankers in Europe and this country, that the safest use of money is in re-discounting bank's bills-receivable taken in the ordinary course of business, with the indorsement of the bank added thereto. This is the kind of loans the clearing houses would accept, and in the estimation of bankers such loans would be considered the best that could be made. They would be based upon the choicest and strongest paper in the portfolios of the banks.

It is with the United States now, as it was with France in 1847, that "the essential interests of the country imperiously demand that every bank bill declared to be lawful money shall be able to circulate equally in all parts of the land."

The same thought was forcibly expressed ten years before by Daniel Webster, when he said in his speech delivered September 28, 1837, " I am of opinion, sir, that we want paper of universal credit, and which is convertible into specie at the will of the holder."

This result can be reached by establishing a trusteeship for the public to pass upon and hold the security for the currency issued, and no agency can be better suited to this work than clearing houses incorporated under federal law.

# X

## STATEMENT

MADE BEFORE SUB-COMMITTEE NO. 2 OF THE COMMITTEE ON BANKING AND CURRENCY, ON THE BILL (H. R. 3338) TO INCORPORATE CLEARING HOUSES AND PROVIDE CLEARING HOUSE CURRENCY, ETC. (FROM THE RECORDS OF THE COMMITTEE.)

Thursday, February 20, 1896.

THE sub-committee met at 10.30 A. M. There were present Messrs. Brosius (chairman), Hill, and Cobb of Missouri.

Mr. Theodore Gilman, of New York city, was introduced and made the following statement: —

### STATEMENT.

MR. CHAIRMAN AND GENTLEMEN: The first stated object of the bill is " to protect and support commercial credit, and to equalize rates of interest," and it provides in its first section for the incorporation of individual banks into clearing house associations.

The theory of the bill is that the absence of a means of supporting credit is inherent in a system like that at present existing in our country, which provides only for the incorporation of individual banks, and stops there.

The organization of individual banks forms the basis of a system, but if the banks are not organized with relations to each other, it is a misnomer to call it a system; it is only an agglomeration. Individual banks are organized under the national currency act on an independent basis, and are empowered to take care of themselves and their customers. They are competitive and not mutually supporting; each one is a unit and autonomous, like a petty principality.

We use the term "national banking system" to describe the 4,000 separate banks which are organized under the National Currency Act of 1863. But do they form a system in the sense in which we use that word to describe systems of which the executive, legislative, and judicial branches of the government are examples? Lower and higher officials, elective bodies, and courts make up the gradations of these systems.

## THE OPERATION OF BANKING.

It is evident that a national bank does not cover the whole operation of banking from the creation of debits and credits to their final extinction. The beginning of the operation is in a bank, and it is concluded in a clearing house. The enormous amount of clearings, aggregating fifty thousand millions annually, show the importance of their functions from a money standpoint. But their services cannot be even thus limited, for they provide the daily test of the solvency of every bank and business man in the country; they provide a barometer of the state of credit and the movements of currency, and are the only places where individual banks are brought together and where united action can be secured.

Out of these conditions comes the necessity of mutual agreements and regulations for the government of the business to be transacted, and for the protection of the banks associated in the clearing house. The clearing house must have its articles of association or incorporation under the laws of the different States, its officers and committees, and their duties must be clearly defined. For the protection of the associated banks there must reside somewhere the right and duty to inspect the affairs of any of their number, and even to suspend one from its privileges on specified proofs and charges. These are powers in which not only the associated banks are interested, as the representatives of their many stockholders, but also all the customers of each bank, and the ramifications of these interests in every clearing house as at present constituted stretch far and wide over the whole country. The organization and regulations of clearing houses become, therefore, matters in which the entire country is interested, and in times of commercial disturbance this becomes evident beyond question. At such times the most delicate questions are brought before clearing houses for their decision, and the wisdom of experienced bankers has then the opportunity to render important service in staying incipient panic and in carrying houses and banks over difficulties that are never known outside of banking circles.

### THE PART OF CLEARING HOUSES IN BANKING.

The banking system, therefore, must be considered to include not only banks but clearing houses as well, and though these latter play such an important part in the banking operations of the country, they are not a part of the national banking system, and are not under governmental supervision. The question arises, Can the national system be considered complete until clearing houses are incorporated in it under United States laws and government supervision? To answer this question intelligently we must then take a glance at our national banking system and inquire what are its chief distinguishing characteristics, not only at home, but as compared with the systems of other nations.

It is a remarkable political fact, and one which we do not always fully appreciate or give sufficient weight to, that the United States stands alone among the nations of the earth in having a national system of banking based upon a general law. This situation has been reached as the outgrowth of American institutions, and as the result of political and financial discussions and campaigns conducted with intense excitement on the one hand, and acknowledged ability on the other. Now it must be received as the first article of our financial creed, universally accepted as republican dogma, that banking in this country must be done under a general law.

## PURPOSE AND EFFECT OF A GENERAL BANKING LAW.

The underlying purpose of a general banking law is to form banks for the benefit of the people, and to make all the advantages of the law free to any who comply with its conditions.

The chief effect of a general law is to create a large number of individual banks of moderate capital in all parts of the country. Banks of great capital, sufficient to give a world-wide credit, or to enable them to establish branches in this and other countries, and to issue currency on their own credit, are not contemplated by a general law. Such banks must have special charters and be to some extent monopolies. They are conducted for the privileged owners and not for the people.

In a banking system composed of 4,000 individual banks of equal standing and moderate capital, there must be found some substitute for the great banks of other countries, like the Bank of England or the Bank of France. That these from their central position and commanding capital give a steadiness to the financial affairs of their countries, and that it would be a benefit for our finances to be steadied in the same way, cannot be denied. Our people will, however, neither renounce their approval of general laws, nor their disapproval of a governmental bank. This great need of a balance-wheel in our financial system can be met in entire harmony with republican institutions by another general law which will provide for the incorporation of associated and adjacent banks in clearing house associations, as provided in the bill before us. By means of the provisions which can be incorporated in a general law, the defect of the lack of commanding capital may be obviated, and all the advantages secured which large resources bring, not only for the transaction of current business, but for special emergencies, when united action would be desired to preserve the stability of the financial situation.

The advantages resulting from the joint action of banks may be seen in the union of those of Great Britain in the crisis of 1890, when by concerted action they formed a guarantee fund of £15,000,000 to save the Barings from suspension. By this magnificent energy a panic was avoided which the Bank of England was utterly unable to meet alone. Among MacLeod's reflections on this subject is the following: "To meet such tremendous crises, as all future ones will be, the Bank of England must act together with all the other banks in the country to support the commercial community."

### CLEARING HOUSE CERTIFICATES OF 1893.

The united action of the banks composing the clearing house of New York in 1857, 1860, and 1861, and at various times since then, by the issue of clearing house certificates, of which the last familiar instance was in 1893, proved of the greatest benefit, not only to New York, but to all the country. This action was without any special legal authority, and it is evident that if our clearing houses are incorporated under a general law, and made part of our banking system, we would have the machinery ready for action all over the country to meet any financial crisis, and that not a day's delay need occur before it is announced that adequate provisions have already been made for any emergency. The united action of the associated banks of the United States through their clearing houses would establish credit, and this resource would always be at hand if the clearing houses were incorporated into our banking system by act of Congress. It is to Congress that the country must look for appropriate legislation to include all banking operations under government supervision, so that, in fact as well as in name, we shall have a national banking system.

Republican ideas have thus far controlled the development of our banking system. Under the guidance of the principles contained in the Declaration of Independence the monetary system of the United States has reached a point which is in certain particulars in advance of that of any other nation in the world. In the characteristics of general banking laws, and in governmental inspection and uniform and complete statistical reports, no other country has reached our degree of theoretical advance. We need but to add the capstone of association under a general law with governmental supervision to make our system not only the best in the world, but the most efficient instrument possible for the development of the resources of our land. And this last step is preëminently republican, for it leaves the individual banks free and independent, and yet organizes them into strong bodies by means of incorporated clearing houses. A banking system so formed would last as long as the principles of representative government.

Having thus considered the incorporation of clearing houses under a national law as necessary to complete the national banking system, we will now discuss such incorporation as a measure " to protect and support commercial credit, and equalize rates of interest."

### SAFEGUARDS AGAINST PANICS.

A bill which has this for its first stated object, not only proposes to do that which the entire business community must approve of, but it implies that commercial credit is now unprotected and unsupported, and that there is need of some additional agencies, other than those at present in existence, to fully and perfectly accomplish this most devoutly to be desired result. The argument on which this bill is based is so simple that it can be stated in a single sentence, but the subject is so large that volumes could be written in elucidation of it. In a sentence, it is this: Panics or failures of commercial credit come upon the business community with unwelcome frequency, and an ample safeguard against their destructive effect would be provided by incorporating clearing houses under United States laws, with power to issue currency on pledge of convertible collateral security to banks applying for such accommodation. It is evident also that any system that is able to bear a great strain can with more ease bear a lesser, and if the system of incorporating clearing houses could avert panics, it could also avert money pressures of less magnitude and meet the requirements of busy seasons as well. It would thus attain the great desideratum of equalizing rates of interest throughout the year, and from one end of the country to the other, so that business men should not be compelled to pay high rates of interest for money only because business is brisk, or those in one part of the country be compelled to pay a higher rate of interest than those living in another.

We must here interject a few general remarks. Bankers, as such, have only an indirect concern in the purchase and minting of silver by the government, for they can bank as well on one basis as another, but they justly ask of the government a banking system as nearly perfect as possible. We must also separate the finances of the government from the operations of commercial banks organized under state and national laws. The government does not issue its currency in accordance with the National Banking Act, but on an entirely different principle. All the troubles of the government of the United States with its currency could be remedied in one season by the enactment of a tariff which would produce a revenue greater than the expenses.

Let us now return from this short digression.

As the lesser is contained in the greater, we must consider, for a proper understanding of the objects of this bill, the nature of the failures of commercial credit, called panics, and the two methods of their cure.

### NATURE OF PANICS.

Panics are occasional failures of confidence and are inseparable from an unprotected credit system. The credit system may be said to have begun in England by the chartering of the Bank of England in 1694. Two years later Bank of England notes were at 20 per cent. discount, and the bank stopped payment thereon in coin.[1] So it appears that two years after the modern credit system was established there was a failure of confidence, and we have been having a repetition of the same experience every few years from that time to the present day.

The cause is not far to seek. We give credit to an order or promise to pay of a government, individual, corporation, or bank. A bank will print a circulating note to read: "We promise to pay on demand one dollar," or will receive deposits and promise to pay them on demand, and if we believe the bank can and will do as it promises we give it credit. But we know all the time that the bank only keeps on hand in cash 25 per cent. of its promises to pay. Everybody knows that, but in an intelligent community — and credit is only possible in such — the giving of this credit is accepted and recognized as reasonable and right, and the sufficiency of a reserve of 25 per cent. is believed to be

[1] Adam Smith, book ii. chap. ii.

as good for all practical purposes as keeping in hand the entire amount.

### DANIEL WEBSTER ON CREDIT.

Not only do banks and governments promise to pay money which they have not in hand, but all business is conducted on the principle of a reserve, or, in other words, on the credit system. The merchant, manufacturer, and business men generally, all promise to pay in the future the money proceeds of commodities which are yet unmanufactured and unsold, and enough cash only is kept on hand to meet present requirements. By means of the credit system the amount of business is enormously increased. "Credit," said Daniel Webster, "has done more a thousand times to enrich nations than all the mines of all the world."

But let something unusual happen, — a war or other disaster, — then the insufficiency of the reserve is brought to men's minds with startling vividness. The credit vanishes and fulfillment of the obligation is demanded.

### SILVER SCARE AND VENEZUELA MESSAGE CAUSED PANIC.

A withdrawal of 10 per cent. of deposits is sufficient to throw the whole banking system of the country into confusion. In 1884 the failure of the Metropolitan Bank and other circumstances caused such a withdrawal and the consequent panic. In 1893 the 'silver scare' and in 1895 the Venezuela message did the same thing. These troubles are due not only to the bank failures, the silver question, and the Venezuela message, but to inherent defects in our system. Therefore the true mode of procedure is to cure the system so that it can in the future meet similar emergencies and not be overwhelmed by them.

With only 25 per cent. it is, of course, impossible to pay 100 per cent., and when a panic occurs a struggle to realize on investments takes place, prices fall, payment of debts is demanded, failures are precipitated, and liquidation, which is commercial death and decomposition, ends all. This is a panic, and every such occurrence causes distress to families and sets whole communities back by destroying productive business and obliterating accumulated capital. The loss to this country by the panic of 1837 was then estimated at six thousand million dollars. This was the greatest monetary panic which the world has ever seen.

Every panic brings its losses and restrictions to business by the disarrangement it causes.

### METHODS OF DEALING WITH PANICS.

There are two methods of dealing with panics, one called the restrictive and the other the expansive.

There are some who say there is no need of any regulation of this subject. They say that the debtor class should take care of themselves; that the general public must be educated to recognize that the market for gold or other forms of money is regulated by the same laws as that of any other commodity, and that the mysterious "money question" consists of nothing but the simple circumstance that a man who has promised to deliver a certain amount of money at a specific date is bound to fulfill his contract in the same way as if he had promised to deliver wheat, cotton, or iron.

This argument would be correct if there were no credit system which has been firmly established by two hundred years of business and incorporated into the laws of the country. If commercial transactions were effected by barter, the above view, which is from Mr. Sampson, money writer of the London "Times" in 1873, would be correct. But by law banks are conducted on the credit system, and the law allows them to contract to pay money with only 25 per cent. of their obligation in cash on hand. If it is legal for banks to conduct their affairs on the credit system, and if failures of that system happen periodically, then the law should make provision to meet those failures, so that the credit system may work smoothly, both in times of peace and quiet, and in times of disaster and commotion.

### FORCING LIQUIDATIONS.

The restrictive method is by forcing liquidations. An enforced liquidation is the closing of a financial transaction, not in its natural order (that is, when a favorable market is reached and all parties realize the expected profit), but by an arbitrary demand of a creditor who is not interested in the profit, and who merely wants his money to provide for present and anticipated wants. An arbitrary and enforced liquidation is nearly always at a serious loss. The panic, however, is stopped because enough cash is thereby realized to supply the wants of creditors. So, whenever a panic occurs liquidations are forced on the business community, and the results are failures and their attendant calamities. After the panic prices recover, and the only difference in the situation is that property has changed hands, many who were in affluence are in poverty, and some investors have picked up bargains from which they make a profit.

The chief agents in enforcing and promoting liquidations are banks, because they have had demands on them which they were obliged to meet, and their only resource is to fill up their diminished reserves out of the money held by the general public. They therefore call in their demand loans and refuse to renew maturing paper. This puts the screws on the money market and the life blood of commerce flows into their tills. They do not treat in this way their own customers, but the general public, and for that purpose a bank is careful not to invest its reserve money in the paper or loans of its customers, but of those known to them only by reputation. There is no intention on the part of banks to work any harm to any one, or to interfere with general business in thus withdrawing currency from the general public. The general public is the great reservoir of currency, and the law provides, as the way for replenishing reserves, that a bank shall not discount when its reserve is below the legal limit. This restrictive method of restoring reserves is, therefore, the one appointed by law. The harm and damage is necessary in following out the provisions of the law, and the consciences of bank officers are relieved of all responsibility, even though they see that their acts must cause unnecessary failures.

### BANKS DO NOT SUFFER FROM LIQUIDATION.

On the other hand, banks do not themselves suffer from the operation of liquidations to any appreciable extent. They hold in effect mortgages on the estates of borrowers, and do not make a loss until those estates are exhausted. Consequently the restrictive method, which is death to business men, seems the best and only way to bank officers. Their loans and paper are paid, their dividends continue, and the bankrupted firms and the injury to business are forgotten. The loss resulting from every money panic is incalculable, but it falls on the business community and not on the banks. Consequently, when bank officers are asked to prepare a banking scheme they suggest a plan like that known as the Baltimore plan, which is meant to work for the benefit of banks. It is one under which panics would be sure to happen. But what do banks care for panics when they do not lose money from them? Under the Baltimore plan security for currency was proposed to be abandoned, the banks were to hold the security, and if a panic should come they would simply apply the screws, and soon all would be well except with the unfortunate business community.

The contingency which we are describing is one in which all banks have simultaneously a heavy demand made upon them. Then they make a simultaneous demand upon the general public, and all the floating supply of currency disappears in a day. This must be the result, because under the credit system 25 per cent. of cash is calculated to keep in solvent condition 100 per cent. of liabilities. By the system of reserve cities, the 25 per cent. is reduced so that the actual cash reserve is only about 10 per cent. In this condition of the credit system, as noted above, a demand for only a few per cent. of banking deposits is sufficient to throw the finances of the country into confusion. Such a demand is likely to occur at any time, and experience shows that every few years some new and unexpected combination of events takes place which produces such a demand with its attendant catastrophe.

Excessive restriction of credit, says MacLeod, causes and produces a run for gold, and, we may add, for all currency on a par with gold. Suspension of discounting and calling of loans necessitates a demand for currency to fill the place of the facilities thus withdrawn.

### EXPANSIVE METHOD.

The restrictive method of dealing with such events produces widespread ruin, and we turn therefore to the expansive method to see if better results may not be obtained from it. MacLeod's correlative statement brings us to the consideration of the second method. He says: "In the modern system of dealing with panics, called the expansive method of credit, it is indispensably necessary that there should be some source to create and issue solid credit to sustain solvent houses in a monetary panic." This is in accordance with the often-quoted sentence of the Bullion Report of 1810 to the British Parliament, the greatest financial document which was ever written. "An enlarged accommodation is the true remedy for that occasional failure of confidence to which our system of paper credit is unavoidably exposed." The comment on this passage made by Professor Sumner in his "History of American Currency" is: "The rule of the bullion committee contemplated the loan of notes by a bank whose credit cannot fail in the wildest panic."

This statement of the expansive theory brings us to the consideration of the features of the bill before us, H. R. 3338.

The bill is intended to allay or prevent panics and to equalize interest charges by providing a means whereby banks can meet the demands caused by failures of confidence in the credit system without putting the screws on the business community and thereby precipitating a panic on the country.

It is hardly necessary to attempt to prove that an enlarged accommodation to solvent houses will allay a panic. A panic is caused by the fear that the reserves will be exhausted and that there will not be enough money to meet all demands. If a large amount of fresh money can be had, all fears will be removed. If that amount is practically inexhaustible, then the panic is at an end.

Professor Sumner's comment is correct, that such money must be in the notes of a bank whose credit cannot fail in the wildest panic.

Now we are ready to test the bill before us by these most stringent requirements.

### OLD UNITED STATES BANK.

There is no bank in the United States, and there never again can be, which occupies a commanding position like the old United States Bank or the Bank of France, to which other banks can come and secure assistance on their commercial assets. A large governmental bank has been tried and found wanting in this country.

Few contests short of war were of greater virulence or had a more complete influence on the development of republican thought than that which resulted in the overthrow of the United States Bank. General Jackson wrote that that event was necessary " to preserve the morals of the people, the freedom of the press, and the purity of the elective franchise." Such a bank is monarchical and not republican. The only resource left open to us in this country is to combine our banks into groups, and thus secure a responsibility equal to the aggregate capital of all the associated banks. This can be done by incorporating clearing house associations in the manner described in the bill under a general United States law, which shall give to clearing houses the power needed to issue circulating notes on commercial assets. By this means the banks will be provided with a way by which they may secure circulating notes of a credit so solid that they never can be doubted in the wildest panic. The pressure would then be taken off the business community and placed upon the banks as part of their legitimate work.

### CLEARING HOUSES OF ISSUE.

The incorporation of clearing houses creates a grade of banks with limited and yet higher powers above the ordinary commercial banks who are members of the clearing houses. Clearing houses, by this bill, are intended to be of two grades, — first, ordinary clearing houses, to which any bank throughout the country may belong; and, second, clearing houses of issue, of which there shall be at least one in each State. Any clearing house whose clearings are over $200,000,000 annually may also be made a clearing house of issue. The intention of the bill is only to allow the issue of clearing house currency to be made in the largest financial centres of the country. But it is necessary in any system for a local issue of currency that the boundaries of States shall be recognized. These are not merely geographical; they are political, social, and legal. Business men become accustomed to the laws and courts of their States, and it becomes easier and safer for them to do business within those limitations. Because a State has no large centre of commerce, it should not be deprived of the benefits which would accrue to its people from the establishment of a clearing house of issue within its borders. The regulation of the internal commerce of States is to a large extent in the hands of the separate legislatures. All these considerations point in the direction of making clearing house districts coterminous with state boundaries. Under this bill no State would be without its clearing house of issue, and in the larger States there might be two. It is evident that the combined capital of banks in the separate States when associated in clearing houses would give a basis for solid credit that would be recognized from one end of the land to the other. Thus one element to meet the requirement of undoubted credit would be surely present in the clearing houses of issue proposed in this bill.

STRENGTH OF A CLEARING HOUSE CURRENCY.

Let us therefore inquire what are the elements of strength in a currency issued in this manner.

First. The commercial assets which would be pledged are chiefly the notes of customers and others, discounted by the bank after careful inspection. These notes represent the entire responsibility of the makers, and are a lien on their stock in trade. The loans, bonds, and notes, held by banks, represent the business and property of the borrowers of the country, and should have behind them a large margin of property. The safety of these obligations is shown by the good dividends declared by the banks as the result of the business of lending and discounting.

Second. The second element of strength in a currency so issued is that the notes are advanced only for 75 per cent. of the value of the assets pledged. The collateral is thus strengthened by the equivalent of two more names, the bank making the pledge and the margin of 25 per cent. At this stage the security may be considered equal to four-name paper, — the specific pledge, the responsibility of the maker, the margin, and the responsibility of the bank.

Third. The payment of the notes issued is guaranteed to the holder by all the banks in the clearing house receiving the notes by vote of their boards. The addition of this indorsement gives to the clearing house currency the strength of the combined capital of the associated banks, and adds to the collateral a fifth name which is stronger than all the other four.

Fourth. By the extension of this system over the whole country, the banks of each district would first guarantee their own issues, and the clearing houses in a State the issues in that State, and if that guarantee should not be sufficient, then it is assumed by all the clearing houses organized under this act in all the States and Territories. This would pledge the banking capital of the country for the redemption of the currency issued by the clearing houses, and thus place the responsibility therefor where it belongs — that is, on the capital which is benefited by the issue and on the banks whose business it is to supervise the granting of credits. The addition of these last guarantees adds a sixth, seventh, and eighth name to the security of the paper currency which would thus be issued, and thus raises it to a rank of credit which cannot be reached by any other means short of a government guarantee.

Fifth. Notes issued by one clearing house are to be received in payment of debts through any other, and thus the notes would be maintained at par over the whole country.

The endeavor is to produce in this form of currency as strong a security as the banks of the country can make. There should be no possibility of doubt or chance of difficulty in prompt payment in connection with it. The notes are intended to be such as Professor Sumner describes, "whose credit cannot fail in the wildest panic." Only notes of that description will be sought as a relief in a panic.

The example of clearing houses when they issue certificates during a panic should be taken as conclusive in this matter. The kind of currency they make for themselves is not too good for the public.

THE BALTIMORE PLAN.

The public should be satisfied with nothing less good than that which satisfies the banks. Can banks take the position that when they make a currency for themselves they make it absolutely as good as they can make it, but when they make a currency for the public it need not be so good, and occasional losses on it must be expected? No losses were ever made on clearing house certificates because they are issued on the principles which have been incorporated in this bill. But when an expert appeared before the House Committee on Banking and Currency in December, 1894, to advocate the issue of notes by banks under the Baltimore plan, in which the giving of security is frankly abandoned, he estimated the "annual crop of insolvent notes," to use his own words, at about $2,160,000. This loss under the Baltimore plan is to be carried primarily by the public, and ultimately paid out of the assets of the failed bank. He acknowledges that these notes "might not be redeemed with quite the same promptness as they are under the now existing arrangements," but this he considers a minor difference. But is it so? The title "sound currency" becomes a travesty when applied to such a system.

If the public knows that there is to be expected under any system an annual crop of over two millions of insolvent and defaulted notes, does not that vitiate and taint the whole mass? Does it not require considerable assurance for the banks to send their experts here to advocate a system of note issues on which the profits go to the banks and the losses to the public? No, gentlemen, the country looks to Congress to provide a note circulation on which the losses shall be borne by those who make money out of it, and which shall be so good that the banks themselves shall maintain it at par from one end of the country to the other. This result can be reached by incorporating clearing houses as provided in this bill. A loan committee would then pass upon the sufficiency of any collateral offered as security for currency. The loan committee would be interested in avoiding a loss which if made would fall in part upon their own banks. "The principle of fellowship in business underlying the state bank system," referred to by Hoyt Sherman in his address before the bankers of Iowa in 1894, which worked so well in that system, would also prevent losses from contingent liability under a clearing house system. No bank note circulation should be authorized by Congress which is not good enough for the banks themselves. If the banks wish the privilege of issuing notes, the test of their goodness should be, Will they agree to accept the currency at their own counters always at par? If the answer is No, then the currency is not good enough for the public. It can, of course, be made good enough by putting enough security back of it. Witness the national bank currency which is secured by government bonds.

### A SECURED CURRENCY.

The principle of a secured currency is the second of the accepted doctrines of the financial creed of the United States. It is a principle which cannot be abandoned as long as we have a government of the people, and for the people, and by the people. It has grown out of our republican institutions; it is an integral and necessary part of banking under general laws; a kind of banking which prevails nowhere else but in the United States. It was a new principle when it first took shape in the New York law of 1838; it was incorporated in the charter of the Bank of England in 1844, and has been the basis of the national currency act of this country since 1863. It is futile as well as unsafe for the advocates of miscalled "sound currency" to urge the frank abandonment of that principle, as they have done in the Baltimore plan and in their various publications.

A secured currency merely means a note issue for the redemption of which ample collaterals have been deposited in the hands of a trustee. It might better be called a trustee currency, for all currency is supposed to be secured, and the only difference is in the custodian of the security. Is the custodian the bank which issues the notes, or is it an entirely separate and distinct party acting as trustee for the note-holder?

It is evident that the note-holder requires the services of a trustee. An issue of obligations which is to be divided up among numerous owners is most conveniently made under some form of trust. This is the rule with railroad mortgages. It applies with still greater force to currency. The proposition that the currency of our country shall be issued by numerous banks, and the goodness of each note shall depend on the soundness of its issuer, is entirely inadmissible. As the business of the country demands numerous banks, the soundness of the currency must depend on collateral security placed in the hands of a trustee. If the security is government bonds and the trustee the

Treasurer of the United States, confidence in currency so issued is immediately established.

GOVERNMENT BONDS AS A BASIS FOR CURRENCY.

But there is a radical difficulty with government bonds as the basis of currency. They do not represent the business transactions of the country. They do not represent the commodities to move which currency is wanted, and are therefore inflexible and inelastic. An elastic currency must be issued for the purposes of trade and commerce. When so issued it comes into existence when wanted, and when it has served its purpose it is retired. It is capital created for a temporary purpose. Trade and commerce are represented by the obligations of merchants, therefore the commercial assets of banks are the true basis for the issue of currency, and when so issued the currency is necessarily elastic.

The note-holder cannot inspect the condition of the bank issuing the notes, nor the character of the commercial assets on which the notes are issued. He must take both on faith or credit. The note-holder gives his confidence completely, and he withdraws it in the same way. If there is no trustee to act for him, he must act for himself, and this he does in short order by presenting the notes for redemption. But if there is a trustee to act for him and the trustee holds ample security to protect him, and if any possible loss is protected by adequate guarantees, then his mind is at rest and the notes pass as money without question and are received freely. So the services of a trustee to watch the interests of the public is an absolutely essential feature in any system which is to give a sound currency to the people.

The trustee named in this bill who shall hold the collateral security to the notes to be issued is the clearing house of issue. Of this grade there is provided one for each State, and any clearing house effecting annual clearings of $200,000,000 may become such. The confidence of the people of a State would naturally be given to the clearing house of issue of their own State. State pride would be invoked to keep its management and credit good. Each State would thus have the naming of the trustee who should hold the securities collateral to the notes issued in their own borders. No one could call in question the faithfulness of such a trustee. The provision contained in the tenth section, that the clearing houses of a State are primarily responsible for any loss from the insufficiency of the collateral pledged, would produce such scrutiny and care that it is improbable that there would be any annual crop of insolvent notes, and if any, the amount would be small. The prospect of a contingent liability to loss would be sure to produce caution and conservative action, as was the case with the old state bank system.

### CURRENCY TO BE EVERYWHERE AT PAR.

A currency to be acceptable to the people must be at par in all parts of the country.

This is the third and last article of the short financial creed of the United States. The people demand that the government shall require that all money which it authorizes to be issued shall be maintained at a parity; to the end that each dollar, whatever may be its composition, shall have equal purchasing and debt-paying power with every other dollar, and that no currency shall be issued which is not convertible into coin. In section 12 it is provided that the circulating notes issued in accordance with the provisions of this bill shall be received at par at all the clearing houses organized under this act. Other acts and bills provide that notes shall be good at the counter of the bank issuing them, and that if not paid on demand the bank's assets shall be liquidated and the notes paid out of the proceeds. This would seem to proceed on the assumption that the bank confers a favor on the community by issuing its notes, whereas the fact is that the people confer the favor on the bank by allowing it to issue and circulate its notes as money. If the people give to the banks this opportunity to engage in a productive business, the bank should not only guarantee the public against ultimate loss, but against any delay.

### INSOLVENT NOTES.

Time is money. If a man's solvency depends on the payment of a note and he has the bank bills in hand for that purpose, it is no consolation to be told that the bills are not good now, but are sure to be paid in a year or two by means of a sinking fund or a liquidation. It is a contradiction of terms to speak of a currency that is not good at all times and in all places. The banks should pay the currency of defaulted banks and relieve the public of the annual crop of insolvent notes, and repay themselves from the proceeds of the liquidation. If there were any insolvent notes, they would be the result of errors of judgment on the part of the banks. The banks are in a position to carry such notes with ease, whereas they are a grievous burden to the community. The features of a clearing house currency then are: —

First. Selected commercial assets as collateral.

Second. The issue of circulating notes to be at 75 per cent. of estimated value.

Third. A pledge with a trustee.

Fourth. Convertibility on demand through all clearing houses in the United States.

If it is said that these provisions are too onerous, the reply is that nothing less secure should be authorized by Congress. A single panic is more onerous than any measure of relief which will ward it off. If "an enlarged accommodation is the true remedy for that occasional failure of confidence to which our system of paper credit is unavoidably exposed," that accommodation must be in the "notes of a bank of issue whose credit cannot fail in the wildest panic."

Various objections to this method of issuing currency have been presented and answered, and now let us consider the advantages which the operation of the bill gives both to banks and the community.

### IMMUNITY FROM PANICS.

The chief benefit to both banks and the people is in the immunity from monetary panics which it would secure. A monetary panic is not always a failure of confidence in banks or in the government or in the goodness of the currency. It is often simply an awakening to the fact that depositors have withdrawn currency, and banks generally are too near the point of exhaustion, and that no relief is in sight. A general withdrawal of 10 per cent. would produce this. The incorporation of clearing houses under United States laws, with power to issue a solid currency, would relieve this apprehension. The railway or manufacturing corporation with weekly and monthly pay rolls to meet, and the merchant with his bills and notes to pay, would not have to go into the market and buy currency for their wants or pay extravagant rates for money. All necessity for hoarding currency would be removed, for who would hoard that of which there would always be a plentiful supply on good collaterals? The way our banking system is running now may be compared to an engine without a safety valve. If the engineer will only watch closely enough, and if the steam never rises above the danger point, there is no fear of an explosion. It is against common sense to run an engine without a safety valve, and so the law should provide a safety valve attachment to be put upon banking and commerce, in order that explosions in the form of panics might not be constantly following every increased pressure on the money market. Nor could a farmer successfully cultivate his fields if he were exposed to frequent earthquakes and eruptions. Stability of the earth's surface is not more essential to farming than freedom from the upheavals of financial panics is to trade.

It might be asked why a new method of issuing clearing house currency should be adopted, when banks of the large money centres now may and do issue their clearing house certificates when occasion demands? The answer is that the issuing of clearing house certificates means the paying out of currency to an equal extent; and this is a most dangerous course for interior banks. The currency goes out but never comes back, and serious trouble would thereby be occasioned. But power to issue clearing house currency has the opposite effect. The gold and legal-tender reserve is retained, and the clearing house currency has a local circulation. If used in the purchase of produce, the notes would not perform their circuit before the proceeds of the produce could be in bank to meet them.

#### PROFIT ON CIRCULATION.

In section 9, lines 33 and 34, it is provided that the charges for issues of circulating notes shall be regulated by each clearing house of issue. This places the whole matter of profit on circulation under the control of clearing houses. The profit might be divided between the bank receiving the notes and the clearing house of issue, but it is evident that there would be both accommodation and profit from the issues.

A community of interest among banks such as was successfully in operation under the state bank system of Indiana, Ohio, Iowa, and other States, and is provided in our bill, involves a closer relationship than at present exists among banks. If banks receive at par the clearing house currency issued in other parts of the country from their own, it becomes immediately a practical necessity that representatives of distant banks should meet each other, exchange views, and adopt regulations to govern banking transactions. Also that representatives of banks within clearing house districts should meet at stated times for the same purpose. There would be a practical object in these meetings. Experience would be exchanged, and a mass of information gathered which would promote conservative management.

### STATE AND NATIONAL ASSOCIATIONS.

Provision is therefore made in sections 23 and 24 of this bill for the formation of state and national banking associations. The meetings of state associations and the national convention would give opportunities for accustoming our banks to united action. These unions would strengthen our national life, and in any occasion of great emergency our banks would be trained to use and exercise their power for the public benefit. If the financial sceptre is ever to pass across the Atlantic, our hands must be made ready to hold it.

54TH CONGRESS, 1ST SESSION, H. R. 3338.

In the House of Representatives, January 7, 1896. Read twice, referred to the Committee on Banking and Currency, and ordered to be printed.

Mr. Fairchild (by request) introduced the following bill: —

A bill[1] to protect and support commercial credit, to equalize rates of interest, to provide for the incorporation of clearing houses, to regulate and define their operations, to provide a clearing house currency secured by pledge of commercial assets and the responsibility of the associated banks, and to provide for the circulation and redemption thereof.

*Be it enacted by the Senate and House of Representatives of the United States of America in Congress assembled,* That associations, to be known as clearing houses, for the settlement of money transactions by effecting clearances between banks, and for doing other business for and between banks, not inconsistent with the provisions of this Act, may be formed by any num-

<small>Articles of association.</small>

---

[1] This bill follows in its form and a large part of its phraseology the National Currency Act of 1863, which is based on the banking laws of the various States, and thus constitutes the best model for a general banking law. Some of the sections follow the laws of New York and Iowa. The methods of the New York Clearing House in the issue of clearing house certificates are adapted to the issue of a currency. Slight changes have been made in the original text of the bill to simplify it, and section 11 has been added to endeavor to secure a large mass of gold at no expense to the banks, after the manner of the Bank of France.

ber of banks, not less than five, duly incorporated, either under the national currency Act or under the laws of any State or Territory of which a majority shall be organized under the national currency Act, in any city of not less than six thousand inhabitants, who shall enter into articles of association for the regulation of the business of the association and the conduct of its affairs, which said articles shall be approved by the stockholders of each bank uniting to form the association at a meeting called for the purpose and shall be signed by the officers of each bank by authority conferred upon them to do so by vote of the stockholders, and a copy of them forwarded to the Comptroller of the Currency, to be filed and preserved in his office.

SEC. 2. That the banks uniting to form such an association shall, by their proper officers, make an organization certificate, which shall specify — *Organization certificate.*

First. The name assumed by such association, which name shall be "The Clearing House of (giving the name of the city where located and where its business of effecting clearances shall be carried on)."

Second. The names, the amounts of the capital stock, and the number of shares into which it is divided, of the banks composing the association.

Third. A declaration that said certificate is made to enable such banks to avail themselves of the advantages of this Act.

The said certificate shall be acknowledged before

a judge of some court of record or a notary public, and such certificate, with the acknowledgment thereof authenticated by the seal of such court, shall be transmitted to the Comptroller of the Currency, who shall record and carefully preserve the same in his office. Copies of such certificate, duly certified by the Comptroller and authenticated by his seal of office, shall be legal and sufficient evidence in all courts and places within the United States, or the jurisdiction of the government thereof, of the existence of such association and of every other matter or thing which could be proved by the production of the original certificate.

SEC. 3. That every association formed pursuant to the provisions of this Act shall, from the date of the execution of its organization certificate, be a body corporate, but shall transact no business except such as may be incidental to its organization, and necessarily preliminary, until authorized by the Comptroller of the Currency to commence the business of effecting clearances. Such associations shall have power to adopt a corporate seal and shall have succession by the name designated in its organization certificate for the period of twenty years from its organization, unless sooner dissolved according to the provisions of its articles of association, or by act of the banks owning two thirds of the capital stock represented in the association, or unless the franchise shall be forfeited by a violation of this Act; by such name it may make contracts, sue and be sued, complain and defend in any court of law or equity, as fully as natural persons; it may elect or appoint directors, and by its board of directors appoint a president, vice-president, treasurer, and other officers, define their duties, require bonds of them, and fix the penalty thereof, dismiss said officers, or any of them, at pleasure, appoint others to fill their places, and exercise under this Act all such incidental powers as shall be necessary to carry on the business of a clearing house for the settlement of money transactions by the mutual set-off of debits and credits, commonly called making clearances for banks, and by obtaining and issuing to the banks composing the association notes according to the provisions of this Act, and by acting as trustee for the note-holders in accordance with the provisions of this Act, by receiving and holding in trust securities pledged by the members of the association as collateral to the notes issued to them, to be called "clearing house currency," and by acting for the members of the association in their united capacity when authorized to do so by a majority vote of said members; and its board of directors shall also have power to define and regulate by by-laws not inconsistent with the provisions of this Act the manner in which its directors shall be elected or appointed, its officers appointed, its property transferred, its general business conducted, and all the privileges granted by this Act to associations organized under it shall be exercised and enjoyed; and its usual business shall be transacted at an office or banking house located in the place specified in its organization certificate.

SEC. 4. That the affairs of every association shall be managed by not less than nine directors, one of whom shall be the president, a majority of whom shall be directors in banks, members of the association which are organized under the national currency Act. Every director shall, during his whole term of service, be a citizen of the United States, and at least two thirds of the directors shall have resided in the State, Territory, or district in which such association is located one year next preceding their election as directors, and be residents of same during their continuance in office. Each director when appointed or elected shall take an oath that he will, so far as the duty devolves on him, diligently and honestly administer the affairs of such association and not knowingly violate, or willingly permit to be violated, any of the provisions of this Act, which oath, subscribed by himself and certified by the officer before whom it is taken, shall be immediately transferred to the Comptroller of the Currency, and by him filed and preserved in his office. At the annual meetings there shall be appointed or elected a loan committee, whose duties shall be as described in sections nine and ten of this Act. Members of this committee shall not be eligible for reëlection or reappointment until one year after their terms of office

*Directors.*

*Qualifications of.*

*Oaths of directors.*

*Loan committee.*

*When eligible for reelection.*

shall have expired. They shall be divided into three classes at their first election or appointment, one third shall serve one year, one third two years, and one third three years, and at every election or appointment thereafter they shall be elected or appointed for a term of three years.

<small>Classes of.</small>

SEC. 5. That the directors of any association first elected or appointed shall hold their places until their successors shall be elected and qualified. All subsequent elections shall be held annually on such day in the month of January as may be specified in the articles of association, and directors so elected shall hold their places for one year and until their successors are elected and qualified. But any director having in any manner become disqualified shall thereby vacate his place. Any vacancy in the board shall be filled by appointment by the remaining directors, and any director so appointed shall hold his place until the next election. If from any cause an election of directors shall not be made at the time appointed, the association shall not for that cause be dissolved, but an election may be held on any subsequent day, thirty days' notice thereof in all cases having been given in a newspaper published in the city, town, or county in which the association is located. If the articles of association do not fix the day on which the election shall be held, or if the election should not be held on the day fixed, the day for the election shall be

<small>Tenure of office of directors.</small>

<small>Elections for.</small>

<small>Failure to hold annual election.</small>

designated by the board of directors in their by-laws or otherwise: *Provided*, That if the directors fail to fix the day, as aforesaid, banks representing two thirds of the capital stock represented in the association may.

SEC. 6. That in all elections of directors, and in deciding all questions at meetings of members of the association, each bank member shall be entitled to a representation equal to the minimum number of directors allowed by law to said bank, but no bank organized under a state or territorial law shall be entitled to a greater representation at such meetings than that of a national bank. Directors of a bank who shall be appointed to represent said bank at meetings of the association may vote by proxy duly authorized in writing, but no officer, clerk, teller, or bookkeeper of such association shall act as proxy, and no bank any of whose liabilities are past due and unpaid shall be allowed representation in the board of directors or at the meetings of the association.

<small>Representation of bank members in elections.</small>

<small>Proxies.</small>

SEC. 7. That if, upon a careful examination of the facts so reported, and of any other facts which may come to the knowledge of the Comptroller, whether by means of a special commission appointed by him for the purpose of inquiring into the condition of such association or otherwise, it shall appear that such association is lawfully entitled to commence the business of a clearing house as described in this Act, the Comptroller shall give to such association a certificate,

<small>Comptroller's certificate of authority.</small>

under his hand and official seal, that such association has complied with all the provisions of this Act required to be complied with before being entitled to commence the business of a clearing house under it, and that such association is authorized to commence said business accordingly; and it shall be the duty of the association to cause said certificate to be published in the city or county where the association is located for at least sixty days after the issuing thereof. Publication of certificate.

SEC. 8. That the clearing house association organized under this Act, in the chief commercial city in each State, or in the city most central and convenient for business in each State, or any clearing house so organized effecting bank clearings of over two hundred million dollars annually, to be designated and approved by the Comptroller of the Currency, shall be made a clearing house of issue. And if there shall be more than one clearing house of issue in a State, then the Comptroller of the Currency shall divide the State into clearing house districts, and banks in each State or district shall do business only with the clearing house of issue in their State or district. Clearing houses of issue. One in each State. Any with clearings of over $200,000,000 annually to be clearing houses of issue. Comptroller may divide States with clearing house districts.

SEC. 9. That a clearing house of issue shall be authorized and empowered to receive from its bank members, or from any bank member of a clearing house within its State or district, with the approval of the directors of said clearing house, commercial assets, Powers of clearing house of issue.

promissory notes, bills of exchange, convertible bonds and stocks, and other securities and evidences of debt as collateral security for the circulating notes of the said association to be issued, as provided in this Act, and on the approval of the value of said commercial assets by its loan committee, the said clearing house of issue may deliver to said bank member seventy-five per centum of said value in its said circulating notes as an advance upon said pledged property, and shall require from said bank member its promissory note of equal amount, which note shall be in form as approved by said clearing house of issue. The bank member taking said circulating notes shall engage to redeem them at all times when called upon to do so by the clearing house issuing the notes and to give any additional collateral needed to restore any depreciation in the value of the assets pledged, on demand; and on failure to comply with such demands before the close of business hours of the day when made, said bank member shall be adjudged in default, and shall be thereupon closed pending an examination by a committee from the association which issued the notes. On recommendation by the examining committee, the loan committee shall proceed to liquidate the loan by turning the securities into cash, in accordance with the method provided in section ten. The bank member taking said notes may release its securities from pledge

<small>May receive bank assets as collateral to currency.</small>

<small>May advance 75 per cent. thereon in circulating notes.</small>

<small>Bank member must engage to redeem at all times, and give additional collateral.</small>

<small>Default.</small>

<small>Provisions for liquidating or paying advances.</small>

by depositing with the said clearing house of issue clearing house currency, United States legal-tender notes, or coin certificates, with any charges made by said clearing house of issue, whereupon it shall be entitled to and shall receive all its securities so pledged. The charges shall be regulated by each clearing house of issue. Upon the receipt of such deposit the clearing house of issue shall immediately give notice in a newspaper published in the city, town, or county in which the association is located, which notice shall be published at least once a week for six months successively, that the notes of such bank member will be redeemed at par; and that all the outstanding circulating notes of such bank member must be so presented for redemption within six years from the date of such notice, and all notes which shall not be thus presented for redemption and payment within the time specified in such notice shall cease to be a charge upon the funds in the hands of the clearing house for that purpose. At the expiration of such notice, it shall be lawful for the clearing house of issue to surrender, and such bank member, or their legal representatives, shall be entitled to receive all the money remaining after such redemption, except so much thereof as may be necessary to pay the reasonable expenses chargeable against the said accounts, including the payment for the publication of the above-mentioned notices.

*Charges regulated by each clearing house of issue.*

*Advertisement of redemption of circulating notes.*

*Must be presented in six years.*

*Bank member entitled to receive money remaining after redemption.*

## BILL TO PROTECT CREDIT

Sec. 10. That each bank member taking such circulating notes shall guarantee the clearing house of issue from loss resulting from such issue to them, and in case of a default in the payment of a loan when demanded by the clearing house of issue or of default arising in any other manner, then it shall be the duty of said clearing house of issue to levy upon all the clearing houses in said State or district, in proportion to the capital of their bank members, a sufficient sum to provide for the payment of said loan, which sum shall be held for the payment and redemption of the circulating notes so issued. And if enough money cannot be obtained by such assessments, then it shall be the duty of said clearing house of issue to report to the Comptroller of the Currency the fact of said default, and it shall be his duty to levy a further assessment upon all the clearing houses organized under this Act in all the States and Territories until such sum is secured, in which case the funds so raised by the Comptroller shall be paid by him to the Treasurer of the United States as a special fund to pay the circulating notes of the defaulting bank member, and he shall appoint a receiver for the collateral securities to the loan or loans in default, who shall take possession thereof and turn them into cash and distribute the proceeds to the banks which have contributed to the assessment, and any surplus after reimbursing them their advances shall be handed

*Guarantee of notes by bank member.*

*Guarantee by all banks in State or district.*

*Guarantee by all clearing houses organized under this act.*

*Liquidation of loans by Comptroller.*

over to the bank member in default or its legal representative. But if the assessment by the clearing house of issue on the banks of its State or district is sufficient to provide the needed funds, then the collaterals shall be administered upon and turned into cash by the loan committee or by a liquidating committee of said clearing house of issue and the cash proceeds shall be appropriated as above provided. At no time shall the total amount of such notes issued to any bank member exceed the amount at such time actually paid in of the capital stock of the bank member so applying. And said loan committee are charged with the duty of supervising said loans so as to maintain the margin of value of the collateral security, and shall demand additional securities to make good any depreciation in their value, and they may allow withdrawals and substitutions of securities which shall not diminish the said value. *[Liquidation of loans by clearing house of issue. Amount of circulation obtainable. Duties of loan committees.]*

SEC. 11. That a clearing house of issue shall be authorized and empowered to receive from its bank members, gold coin of the United States of full weight, and may deliver to said bank member its circulating notes at the par of the gold coin so deposited, and the said bank member shall engage to redeem said circulating notes at all times when called upon to do so by the association issuing them. Such notes may be issued to any bank member in exchange for gold coin without regard to the amount *[U. S. gold coin to be accepted at par and notes issued thereon.]*

of the capital stock of the bank depositing the gold coin. The clearing house of issue shall make report of notes so issued to the Comptroller of the Currency and shall make no charge for the issue of its notes against the deposit of gold.

Sec. 12. That in order to furnish suitable notes for circulation, as provided in this Act, the Comptroller of the Currency is hereby authorized and required, under the direction of the Secretary of the Treasury, to cause plates and dies to be engraved, in the best manner, to guard against counterfeiting and fraudulent alterations, and to have printed therefrom, and numbered, such quantity of circulating notes, in blank, of the denominations of one dollar, two dollars, five dollars, ten dollars, twenty dollars, fifty dollars, one hundred dollars, five hundred dollars, and one thousand dollars, as may be required to supply under this Act the associations entitled to receive the same, which notes shall express upon their face that they are secured by deposit with the clearing house of issue at (naming the city) of commercial assets at seventy-five per centum of their market value, and that said clearing house holds said assets as trustee for the note-holder to secure their payment, which payment is guaranteed by the associated banks of the United States through any clearing house, and shall be attested by the signatures of the president or vice-president and treasurer of said clearing house of issue as for account of the bank member receiving

*Preparation of clearing house currency.*

*What note shall express.*

*Payment guaranteed by the associated banks of the U. S. through any clearing house.*

said notes, and on requisition of a clearing house of issue the Comptroller of the Currency shall forward the amount of blank notes in denominations as called for as may be required to supply the bank member entitled to receive the same under this Act.

*Comptroller shall furnish notes.*

SEC. 13. That after any such clearing house of issue shall have caused its promises to pay such notes on demand to be signed by the president or vice-president and treasurer thereof, in such manner as to make them obligatory promissory notes, payable on demand, such clearing house of issue shall deliver them to the bank member entitled to receive them, who is hereby authorized to issue and circulate the same as money, and the same shall be received at par at all the clearing houses in the United States organized under this Act, and said clearing house of issue shall thereupon forward to the Comptroller of the Currency a certificate setting forth the amount of notes delivered, the name of the bank member receiving same, and the amount of the collateral security held in trust for their redemption.

*Notes for what and how receivable.*

*Amount of notes delivered to be certified to Comptroller, also collateral security.*

SEC. 14. That it shall be the duty of the clearing house of issue to receive worn-out or mutilated circulating notes issued by it to any bank member, and also, on due proof of the destruction of any such circulating notes, to deliver in place thereof other circulating notes of like tenor and amount. And such worn-out or mutilated notes, after a memorandum shall have

*Worn out or mutilated circulations.*

been entered in the proper books, as may be established by the clearing house of issue, as well as all circulating notes which shall have been paid or surrendered to be canceled, shall be burned to ashes in presence of three persons, one to be appointed by the Comptroller of the Currency, one by the clearing house of issue, and one by the bank member on whose account they were issued, and a certificate of such burning shall be made on the books of the clearing house of issue, and duplicates forwarded to the Comptroller of the Currency and to the bank member whose notes are thus canceled.

SEC. 15. That it shall be unlawful for any officer acting under the provisions of this Act to countersign or deliver to any association or to any other company or persons any circulating notes contemplated by this Act, except as hereinbefore provided and in accordance with the true intent and meaning of this Act. Any officer who shall violate the provisions of this section shall be deemed guilty of a high misdemeanor, and on conviction thereof shall be punished by fine not exceeding double the amount so countersigned and delivered and imprisonment not less than one year and not exceeding fifteen years, at the discretion of the court in which he shall be tried.

<small>Penalty for improper delivery of notes.</small>

SEC. 16. That it shall be lawful for any such association to purchase, hold, and convey real estate as follows:—

<small>Real estate.</small>

First. Such as shall be necessary for its immediate accommodation in the transaction of its business.

Second. Such as shall be mortgaged to it in good faith by way of security for debts previously contracted.

Third. Such as shall be conveyed in satisfaction of debts previously contracted in the course of its dealings.

Fourth. Such as it shall purchase at sales under judgment, decrees, or mortgages held by such association, or shall purchase to secure debts due to said association.

Such association shall not purchase or hold real estate in any other case or for any other purpose than as specified in this section, nor shall it hold the possession of any real estate under mortgage, or hold the title and possession of any real estate purchased to secure any debts due to it for a longer period than five years.

SEC. 17. That the plates and special dies to be procured by the Comptroller of the Currency for the printing of such circulating notes shall remain under his control and direction, and the expense necessarily incurred in executing the provisions of this Act, respecting the procuring of such notes and all other expenses of the bureau, shall be assessed each year upon the clearing houses organized under this Act, in proportion to the capital stock of their members. *Control of plates and dies.* *Expenses assessed on clearing houses.*

SEC. 18. That the Comptroller of the Currency, with the approbation of the Secretary of the Treasury, as often as shall be deemed necessary or proper or at the request of *Clearing house examiners.*

any clearing house, shall appoint a suitable person or persons to make an examination of the affairs of every association organized under this Act, which person shall not be a director or other officer in any association whose affairs he shall be appointed to examine, and who shall have power to make a thorough examination into all the affairs of the association, and in doing so to examine any of the officers and agents thereof on oath, and shall make a full and detailed report of the condition of the association to the Comptroller, who shall fix the compensation for his services.

SEC. 19. That every president, director, treasurer, teller, clerk, or agent of any association who shall embezzle, abstract, or willfully misapply any of the moneys, funds, or credits of the association, or shall, without authority from the directors, issue or put in circulation any of the notes of the association, or shall, without such authority, assign any note, bond, draft, bill of exchange, mortgage, judgment, or decree, or shall make any false entry in any book, report, or statement of the association with intent in either case to injure or defraud the association, or any other company, body politic or corporate, or any individual person, or to deceive any officer of the association, or any agent appointed to examine the affairs of any such association, shall be deemed guilty of a misdemeanor, and upon conviction thereof shall be punished by imprisonment not less than five nor more than ten years.

*Penalty for official malfeasance.*

SEC. 20. That every person who shall mutilate,

cut, deface, disfigure, or perforate with holes, or shall unite or cement together, or do any other thing to any note issued by any such association, or shall cause or procure the same to be done, with intent to render such note unfit to be reissued by said association, shall, upon conviction, forfeit fifty dollars to the association who shall be injured thereby, to be recovered by action in any court having jurisdiction. *Penalty for mutilating currency.*

SEC. 21. That if any person shall falsely make, forge, or counterfeit, or cause or procure to be made, forged, or counterfeited, or willingly aid or assist in falsely making, forging, or counterfeiting, any note in imitation of, or purporting to be in imitation of, the circulating notes issued under the provisions of this Act, or shall pass, utter, or publish, or attempt to pass, utter, or publish, any false, forged, or counterfeited note, purporting to be issued by any association doing business under the provisions of this Act, knowing the same to be falsely made, forged, or counterfeited, or shall falsely alter, or cause or procure to be falsely altered, or willingly aid or assist in falsely altering, any such circulating notes, issued as aforesaid, or shall pass, utter, or publish, or attempt to pass, utter, or publish, as true, any falsely altered or spurious circulating note issued, or purporting to have been issued, as aforesaid, knowing the same to be falsely altered or spurious, every such person shall be deemed and adjudged guilty of felony, and being thereof convicted by due course of law shall be sentenced to be impris- *Penalty for counterfeiting circulation.*

oned and kept at hard labor for a period of not less than five years nor more than fifteen years, and fined in a sum not exceeding one thousand dollars.

SEC. 22. That if any person shall make or en-
<small>Penalty for illegal possession or use of material for circulation.</small> grave, or cause or procure to be made or engraved, or shall have in his custody or possession any plate, die, or block after the similitude of any plate, die, or block from which any circulating notes, issued as aforesaid, shall have been prepared or printed, with intent to use such plate, die, or block, or cause or suffer the same to be used, in forging or counterfeiting any of the notes issued as aforesaid, or shall have in his custody or possession any blank note or notes engraved and printed after the similitude of any notes issued as aforesaid, with intent to use such blanks, or cause or suffer the same to be used, in forging or counterfeiting any of the notes issued as aforesaid, or shall have in his custody or possession any paper adapted to the making of such notes, and similar to the paper upon which any such notes shall have been issued, with intent to use such paper, or cause or suffer the same to be used, in forging or counterfeiting any of the notes issued as aforesaid, every such person, being thereof convicted by due course of law shall be sentenced to be imprisoned and kept to hard labor for a term not less than five or more than fifteen years, and fined in the sum not exceeding one thousand dollars.

SEC. 23. That it shall be the duty of the Comp-

troller of the Currency to report annually to Congress at the commencement of its session : — *Annual report.*

First. A summary of the operations and condition of every association from whom reports have been received the preceding year, at the several dates to which such reports refer, with an abstract of the whole amount of their debts and liabilities, the amount of circulating notes outstanding, and the total amount of means and resources, specifying the amount of lawful money held by them at the times of their several returns, and such other information in relation to said associations as in his judgment may be useful.

Second. A statement of associations whose business has been closed during the year, with the amount of their circulation redeemed and amount outstanding.

Third. Any amendment to the laws relative to clearing houses, by which the system may be improved, and the security of the holders of their notes may be increased.

Fourth. The whole amount of the expenses of carrying out the provisions of this Act. And such report shall be made by or before the first day of December in each year, and the usual number of copies, for the use of the Senate and House, and one thousand for the use of the Department, shall be printed by the Public Printer and in readiness for distribution at the first meeting of Congress.

SEC. 24. That the clearing houses organized under this Act may organize among themselves

150    BILL TO PROTECT CREDIT

associations to include the bank members thereof in any State or district and may hold annual conventions and meetings at other times, for the formulation of rules and regulations for the conduct of their affairs and for the discussion of financial subjects and for the preservation and exchange of information to govern the granting of credits, and when approved by the Secretary of the Treasury, such rules and regulations shall be binding upon the banks and clearing houses within said State and district.

<small>State bankers' associations.</small>

SEC. 25. That clearing houses organized under this Act may form a national association, which shall meet in convention annually, and whose object shall be the promotion of the interests of the banks of the United States receiving the benefits of this Act, and said convention may pass rules and regulations to govern the operations of clearing houses and the banks connected with same, which, when approved by the Secretary of the Treasury, shall be binding upon such clearing houses. The delegates to a State or district convention shall number one hundred, and to a general convention three hundred, which numbers divided into the aggregate of the banking capital represented will give in each case the amount of capital to be taken as the basis of representation. The Comptroller of the Currency may unite banks into voting groups where their separate capital is below the basis of representation, and each group shall be entitled to one representative. All elections of representatives to conventions shall be by

<small>National bankers' association.</small>

a majority vote of the directors entitled to vote of single banks and banks composing groups; each bank shall have a vote equal to the minimum number of directors allowed to it by law; but no bank shall be allowed more votes than shall be given to a national bank, and no bank shall have more than one representative in the national association.

# XI

## THE COMPLETION OF THE NATIONAL BANKING SYSTEM [1]

THE INCORPORATION OF CLEARING HOUSES UNDER UNITED STATES CHARTERS, WITH ADDITIONAL POWERS AND DUTIES; AND THE ISSUE OF A CLEARING HOUSE CURRENCY, AS A MEANS OF PREVENTING MONEY PANICS

### THE PANIC OF 1893 A TEST PERIOD.

THE system of banking prevailing in this country under the laws of Congress is now passing through a test period. A test involves a strain greater than is required for work done under ordinary conditions. No system can be considered perfect which breaks down when put to the test. Our banking laws on the one hand invite the investment of capital in a business which is intended to be so surrounded by legal safeguards that the risk is supposed to be small to those who act strictly within the provisions of the law. On the other hand, the law invites the people to deposit their money with the banks because the safeguards are assumed to be sufficient for their protection. Experience has shown that under ordinary conditions our national banking system works well and shows no appearance of defective theories, but that under

[1] Reprinted from the *Bankers' Magazine*, September, 1893.

# A LACK OF CONFIDENCE 153

the stress of severe and protracted strain it fails unmistakably to accomplish some of the results for which it was designed.

### NATIONAL BANKING ACT AFFORDS INSUFFICIENT PROTECTION.

The present financial disturbance is marked by one distinguishing characteristic, which is a lack of confidence both on the part of the banks and of depositors in the provisions of the law for their protection. And this lack of confidence is well founded. A bank conducted in strict compliance with the law as to reserves and investments, and honestly and prudently managed, with not a single weak asset on its books, could not hope to withstand successfully unusual demands like those of the past few weeks without outside assistance. The perception of this fact by the depositing public was enough to produce a money panic. Bank officers and the public alike see that the ordinary provisions of the law are inadequate to protect either the capital invested under the sanction of the law and in compliance therewith, or the depositors who rely thereon. The panic is therefore rational, for it is based on facts which justify it. Numerous suspensions and failures have taken place by which depositors will not ultimately lose anything, because the banks are said to be sound and well managed. Here, then, we have loss of credit, distress, derangement of business, and every evil which can come from a bank failure or suspension, except loss to depositors ; and yet there has been no infringement of the law, or business mistakes, or even errors of judgment. Though there were none of these, and the compliance with the law has been perfect, yet the result has been disaster.

### A WELL-SECURED RESERVE SHOULD BE PROVIDED BY LAW.

It is, therefore, a matter of common honesty and fair dealing with the stockholders of national banks to change the provisions of the law so that even under the stress of the greatest strain that can be imagined, it shall be sufficient for their complete and perfect protection. It is an exceedingly simple and easy matter to accomplish this; but it is not at all simple to do so in a way that will leave the banks in a position to earn a fair return upon their capital. If the reserve limit were raised to 75 per cent., all to be kept in the bank's own vaults, we should of course hear no more of bank failures. But under such a restriction most banks would retire from business, because it would thereby be made unprofitable. To maintain such a large amount of capital in perpetual idleness would entail a great loss of productive power to the community. It would be like the policy of keeping a large standing army at all times, instead of a militia which can be called out when needed. What is wanted is, therefore, not more idle capital, but a well-secured reserve which can be relied on in case of necessity, and can be retired, when it has rendered its service, leaving the small regular reserves on duty on a peace footing. This is the application to business affairs of the methods which have been found both economical and effective in the government of a State.

## INCORPORATION OF CLEARING HOUSES UNDER A FEDERAL LAW.

The banks of New York city have established a mode of meeting a crisis which is at once effective and simple, by the use of clearing house certificates. These certificates form a currency among the members of the clearing house which is accepted by them in payment of debts due each other. It is only necessary to legalize and extend that which is now done extra-legally, to afford instant relief to the whole banking and business community. This could be accomplished by a law in Congress incorporating clearing houses. These institutions are a necessary part of the national banking system, and, as such, they should have a uniform method of operation, and derive their powers from the national government. All the national banks in the country might be included in clearing house districts, and banks organized under state laws might also be members. All their powers and privileges would be specified and regulated by the law, and among these should be the power to issue clearing house legal tenders. This power should be limited to those whose clearings were the largest, say $500,000,000 per annum or over. These clearing house legal tenders should not only be a currency between banks but for the people as well. They should be a legal tender for the payment of debts at all clearing houses, thus maintaining them at par throughout the whole country; and they should be counted by banks holding them as part of their reserves. The amount of the reserve provided for by the clearing house legal tenders should be large enough to make the provision adequate for all possible requirements. The present legal reserve is 25 per cent., and the maximum of the reserve thus provided should be 25 per cent. more. The banks would thus possess a reserve of 50 per cent. immediately available, of which 25 per cent. would be active and 25 per cent. latent, but ready to come into existence at short notice. A 50 per cent. reserve would be sufficient to meet and overcome the severest panics this country has known. The effect of the possession of this power by the banks would necessarily be that the danger of a money panic would be forever removed. The power to make such issues would stamp out forever the fear that a crisis would or might occur when the banks would not have enough money to "go around." The power to produce disaster by hoarding currency, which is now possessed by timorous or evil-minded men, would be forever taken away.

### SECURITY FOR CLEARING HOUSE CURRENCY.

These new legal tenders would be secured, as clearing house certificates now are, by pledge of bank assets at 75 per cent. of their value, and guaranteed by all the banks of all the clearing houses, the members of each clearing house being the first guarantors of their own issues. They would be issued in conformity to the financial principle recognized by all authorities, and well stated by Charles Moran in his book on "Money" (1863), page 110, as follows: "Paper money to perform successfully the functions of money should never be issued except against a pledge, direct or indirect, of a greater value of useful commodities, needed by the community, applicable to the redemption of the bank notes issued." A six per cent. rate of interest to banks taking clearing house legal tenders would act as a check upon their issue, and they would not be taken so much for profit as for protection and necessity. The interest on the notes of the banks applying for the currency would accrue to the clearing houses to form a fund to meet such obligations as they might have. Such legal tenders would be intended to perform a temporary service, and provision should be made for the comptroller to call for their retirement in installments of a certain percentage at specified times. The time they should be allowed to remain out might extend over six to nine months to permit settlements to be made and other liquidations from sales of securities, produce, and merchandise. If cash for their redemption was not provided by the borrowing banks, or by sale of the assets pledged, then the resulting loss should be assessed first on the banks in the districts making the issues, and thereafter on all national banks in proportion.

### IMMUNITY FROM PANIC.

Immunity from the disasters which result from a money panic is a protection demanded by justice, and should be given by law to the banking corporations which the law creates. As the experience of every panic proves that the present provisions of the banking law are inadequate to give that protection, then whatever remedy experience shows is effective should be incorporated in the law. The experience of New York in the use of clearing house certificates shows that they are effective and safe in their final results.

#### THE ENTIRE COUNTRY INTERESTED IN STABILITY.

It is to be remembered that such measures have their effect, not only on national banks, but also on all the financial interests of the country which rest upon the deposit banks as their foundation. The deposit banks are the great balance wheel of the country. On their orderly movement depends in a great measure the safety of the savings banks and the commercial community. The present disturbance has thus far affected only the deposit banks, but if not arrested it may extend to the depositors in savings banks. If these are seized with any unreasoning fear, which now may be brewing, and the burden of providing for ten per cent. of these deposits, or even a hundred millions of them, be added to present requirements, it is evident that a general collapse and prostration of the entire business interests of the nation might ensue.

The entire community is therefore interested in any attempt to perfect and complete the national banking system, because in proportion as such efforts are successful the material interests of the whole country are promoted.

NEW YORK, July 25, 1893.

# XII

### FIXED AND REDEEMABLE CURRENCY[1]

#### FUNDAMENTAL PRINCIPLES MUST BE ESTABLISHED.

THE present discussion of the currency question cannot be brought to a satisfactory conclusion until an agreement is reached as to fundamental principles. The following pages are written with a desire to bring about such an agreement, and thus to make concerted action possible.

#### METAL AND PAPER CURRENCY.

There are two materials used as currency, metal and paper. Metal currency may be called fixed, because when the precious metals are minted into coins, they become practically fixed and permanent in shape and value. They do not rust, they do not lose their value in fire, and the process of abrasion is so slow that it proves their permanent character. Paper currency from its nature must be redeemable, for fire consumes it, water dissolves it, attrition destroys it, and age fades it. Being of a perishable character and of no intrinsic worth, its value must be found in that by which it is to be redeemed.

[1] Reprinted from the *Bankers' Magazine*, October, 1893.

## FIXED AND REDEEMABLE CURRENCY.

Currency is therefore naturally and truly divided into two classes, fixed and redeemable.

### FIXED CURRENCY.

Fixed currency is exchangeable, but not redeemable, unless exchange be considered a form of redemption. It is exchangeable because it has intrinsic value, and every act of exchange is a renewed confirmation of its value. There can be but one measure of value, and the metal least liable to fluctuate is the best for that use. The metal has cost a certain amount of labor to mine and mint, and that is the measure of its value.

The precious metals when coined have three characteristics. They are currency, capital, and commodity: currency, because they are accepted in exchanges at a certain value that is stamped upon them; capital, because they are the produce of industry which may be used in facilitating production; and a commodity, because they have what is called intrinsic value. All these three qualities are present in fixed currency at all times, but when effecting exchanges, it is' capital and commodity used as currency; when held as reserve, it is a currency and a commodity used as capital; when wanted for neither purpose, it is a currency and capital which can only be used as a commodity. The laws of trade, which are superior to and cannot be controlled by the laws of either states or nations, determine how much fixed currency is needed for effecting exchanges, how much as capital, and what amount is only a commodity. The law of parsimony fixes the first two amounts at the smallest which will perform the required services, and the last at the largest amount which can be spared, because it is idle capital. As business is the mind and muscle of man engaged in productive labor, the endeavor is to keep labor and the results of labor in active operation. Idle capital is therefore as abhorrent to a business man as a vacuum has been said to be to nature. If idle capital in the shape of fixed currency cannot be employed at home, it is sure to be exported for the payment of foreign debts, or for investment in home or foreign securities. The coins held by individuals and banks are merely a convenience in effecting exchanges and paying debts, domestic and foreign. No one wants more coins than are sufficient for these purposes. If one has more, he immediately seeks methods of exchanging them for some form of productive capital.

### THE AMOUNT OF FIXED CURRENCY REGULATED BY THE LAWS OF TRADE.

As the amount of fixed currency in a country is therefore regulated by certain immutable laws, any variation either in the direction of enforced scarcity or of redundance is sure to produce the bad results which invariably follow the infraction of natural laws. If the coin is debased, it will drive out of the country the coin which has greater value but is stamped as of equal value with it. If a larger amount is coined than is required, the surplus will surely flow abroad.

The needs of one country vary from those of another. Great extent of territory, distance of financial centres from each other, wealth of inhabitants per capita, activity of business operations, nature of business done, and other considerations, all go to determine the amount of fixed currency needed by a country. While good estimates may be made as to the amount required, only the needs of the people as developed and ascertained by actual business can fix the limit; the method is practical, not theoretical. If there is too little currency, the country will call loudly for more. If there is too much, it will ship the surplus abroad.

#### FIXED CURRENCY IS "SOUND."

Fixed currency has the great advantage over every other form in that there is no question as to its "soundness." It is tangible, and makes no appeal to the confidence of the user. An illiterate man or a savage knows that it is good when he sees it.

#### PAPER CURRENCY RESTS ON CONFIDENCE.

Paper currency, on the contrary, rests entirely on the confidence of the community. It is a currency, because it is accepted at the value printed upon it, and it represents capital and commodities. It differs from metal currency in that it is representative and redeemable. Being representative, it is a convenient and cheap substitute for metal;

being redeemable, it need never be idle. When it has performed its service and has no more work to do, it can be redeemed and canceled. It is a promise to pay, and making no pretense to intrinsic worth, its whole value lies in the credit of the issuer and in the value of the property pledged to secure its payment. But being so economical, serviceable, portable, and convenient, all civilized communities find its use in some form a commercial necessity.

**PAPER CURRENCY MAY BE COVERED WITH COIN.**

Paper may be issued on the deposit of an equal amount of coin, in which case its only, but very great advantage, is its portability. Paper of this kind is in all points similar to metal currency, and is governed by the same laws.

**PAPER CURRENCY MAY BE SECURED BY BONDS.**

Paper currency may be issued against pledge of government bonds, as our present national bank currency is, in which case it releases the capital invested in such bonds before the date of their maturity. As this operation gives a small profit to the banks, they become purchasers of these bonds and sustain their price in times of commercial depression or in a time of war. The national banking currency therefore simply anticipates the payment of the bonds issued by the government. When the bonds mature and are paid, then gold will take the place of the national bank notes, and the volume of the currency will to that extent only change its form, and not necessarily be diminished in amount by the disappearance of the bank notes. The payment of the bonds by the government in gold at their maturity would ordinarily be a stimulus to business, but having discounted the bonds, we have eaten our cake, and manifestly we cannot have it at the same time.

### BENEFITS OF NATIONAL BANK CURRENCY THREEFOLD.

The national currency is therefore a benefit to the government in providing a purchaser for its bonds, a benefit to the banks in giving them a profit on the circulation, and a benefit to the country in discounting the payment of the bonds. There is no necessity to provide a substitute for national banking currency, as we often hear urged. The government provides the substitute in the gold with which it will pay the bonds. The money will go into the hands of the United States Treasurer to redeem the national banking currency, any surplus will go to the banks, the profit on currency will cease with the stoppage of interest on the bonds, and the bond-currency transaction will be closed. It will have served an excellent purpose and have been a great benefit to all parties concerned.

It is evident that such a currency transaction as this is a special one, and cannot be repeated until the government shall again need the aid of the banks in floating its bonds, which event we may hope will never recur.

## GOVERNMENT NOTES A FORM OF FIXED CURRENCY.

Government or "fiat" notes are a form of fixed currency, and as such should be instantly convertible into coin. If they are not, the measure of value becomes a fluctuating one, which is inconsistent with commercial integrity. " Divers weights are an abomination unto the Lord." The government can legally issue its fixed currency, but it is morally bound to keep it at par with coin, and its function is rather to regulate the currency than to issue it for a profit. The proposition that the government shall issue all the currency is one that cannot be entertained or discussed. The debate on this subject was closed a hundred years ago, and since then all have been ready for " the question." It must be simply voted down. The minority in favor of a " fiat" currency is too small to make it a live issue.

### REDEEMABLE CURRENCY.

From the foregoing it appears that paper currency issued against deposit of precious metals or government bonds, and government " fiat" notes, are only other forms of fixed currency. The paper represents either a dollar of coin or the promise of the government to pay a dollar at some future time.

### PAPER CURRENCY ISSUED ON COMMERCIAL ASSETS.

We have, therefore, thus far been considering fixed currency only, in the form of metal coins, paper issued against metal, and paper issued against the government promise to pay coin. If, however, paper can be issued with advantage against pledge of coin or government bonds for its redemption, why cannot it be issued against other commodities and securities which have a recognized value and which in ordinary process of business will find a market, be exchanged for money, and thus provide the cash with which to redeem the paper money which has been issued against the commodities and securities? Is silver or gold any safer as a security for currency than other products of the mine, copper, iron, lead, petroleum, and coal; or than agricultural products, wheat, corn, and cotton; or than manufactured goods, flour, provisions, and cotton goods; or than the stocks and bonds of municipalities and corporations whose credit is unquestioned; or than the bills receivable of business firms and corporations which represent and are based upon all these commodities and securities? It is evident that if the government should experience an important benefit from the monopoly of the banking currency of the country, then these other varied interests represented by the products of labor would receive a corresponding benefit if they could by any means be used as the basis for the issue of currency.

### SAFEGUARDS REQUIRED.

But when the issue of paper currency against the pledge of other forms of property than the precious metals or government securities is proposed, immediately many considerations arise which did not before require attention.

The chief consideration, which lies at the foundation of the reluctance of the public to commit itself to any particular currency measure, is that the country demands that its currency shall be safe and worthy of confidence not only at home but throughout the world. Public opinion will not tolerate any doubt on this subject, and it is unwilling to take chances in connection with it. Any scheme which is proposed must therefore be able to stand all the tests which ingenuity and experience can bring to bear against it.

### THE FUNCTION OF PAPER CURRENCY TO EFFECT EXCHANGES.

The function of a redeemable paper currency is to effect exchanges and not to supply a medium of intrinsic value. Such a system is only a machine for effecting exchanges. It must first be safe, or it will be useless. The idea of safety is fundamental, but we must first say a word regarding its nature and functions.

### MUST THEN BE BASED ON COMMODITIES TO BE EXCHANGED.

If a redeemable paper currency is used to effect exchanges, then it should be based on the commodities which are to be exchanged, and the closer it can be brought under the control of the banks through whom the exchanges are effected, and the nearer it can be made to conform to the wants of business men who effect the exchanges, the more serviceable and efficient does the machine become. Exchangeability or convertibility, then, should be the test of property to be used as a basis for a redeemable circulation. As the notes are demand obligations, quick convertibility is also an absolute requirement in all collaterals pledged for an issue of bank notes. This requirement would exclude real estate and all other slow assets which are sufficiently provided for by the money of savings banks and trust estates.

### PAPER CURRENCY MUST BE SAFE.

If a redeemable currency would be beneficial to the business of the country and to the debtor class, and if it may properly be based upon bankable assets, the remaining requirements are that any scheme for its issue shall be safe beyond contingency, and that the currency shall be maintained over the whole country at par.

### HOW SAFETY MAY BE ATTAINED.

These two points would be secured by adopting as a model the main features of the certificates issued by the New York Clearing House. The mode of their issue is the result of the experience of the officers of banks which do a large business and are managed conservatively. They endeavored to produce in these certificates as strong a security as the banks of New York could make. There was to be no possibility of doubt or chance of difficulty in connection with them. If, therefore, such a system could be extended over the whole country, it would furnish a currency as strong as the united banks of the country could make. It is not easy to conceive of a stronger currency than one issued under the supervision of clearing houses to the banks which are their accredited members, under restrictions and regulations imposed by a law of Congress.

#### FIVE ELEMENTS OF STRENGTH IN CLEARING HOUSE CURRENCY.

Let us, therefore, inquire what are the elements of strength in these certificates, and from that will appear what would be the strength of a currency issued in like manner.

#### BASED ON THE BUSINESS OF THE COUNTRY.

First. Clearing house certificates are based primarily on the notes of the customers of the banks, which are the underlying obligations that the banks take in making a discount. One of these notes represents the entire responsibility of the customer, and it is a lien on his stock in trade. Usually this is fortified also by indorsements or a pledge of collateral. The loans and notes held by banks, therefore, represent the business and property of the borrowers of the country, and each should have behind it a large margin of property. The safety of these obligations is shown by the good dividends declared by the banks as the result of the business of lending and discounting. They represent the active business men and the commercial enterprises of the country.

#### ISSUED AT 75 PER CENT. OF COLLATERAL.

Second. The second element of strength in these certificates is that they are issued to banks only, at 75 per cent. of the par value of the notes and other securities pledged. The collateral to the certificates is thus strengthened by the equivalent of two more names, the bank making the pledge and the margin of 25 per cent. At this stage the security may be considered equal to four-name paper, each name being strong and separate.

Proposals that banks should give security for their issues have been discussed for fifty years. The principle has been the foundation of our national banking currency, is an essential feature of clearing house certificates, and should be incorporated in whatever new currency system is established hereafter. McCulloch [1] writes in an interesting discussion, which is closely applicable to the present times: " Had this principle been adopted, the presumption is that the crisis of 1837–39 would have been obviated or materially mitigated."

#### GUARANTEED FIRST BY LOCAL CLEARING HOUSE.

Third. The payment of the principal and interest of the certificates is also guaranteed to the holder by all the banks of the clearing house by vote of their boards. The addition of this indorsement gives to the certificates the strength of the combined capital of all the associated banks

---

[1] See his argument on this subject, pages 502, 503 of his fifth edition of Adam Smith's *Wealth of Nations*.

and adds to the collateral a fifth name, which is stronger than all the other four.

GUARANTEED BY ALL THE CLEARING HOUSES OF THE COUNTRY.

Fourth. The extension of this system over the whole country and its adaptation to the issue of currency instead of certificates, is only the development of a plan which has been found by practical experience to be good. The whole country would be divided into clearing house districts, and all banks of each district should first guarantee their own issues, as is done by the New York associated banks, and thereafter the issues of the others. This would pledge the banking capital of the country for the redemption of the currency issued by the clearing houses, and thus place the responsibility therefor where it belongs, — that is, on the capital which is benefited by the issue, and on the banks, whose business it is to supervise the granting of credits. The addition of this last guarantee adds a sixth name to the security of the paper currency which would thus be issued, and as it is stronger than all the other five, it raises such currency to a rank of credit which cannot be reached by any other means short of a government guarantee.

MAINTAINED AT PAR OVER THE WHOLE COUNTRY.

Fifth. Notes issued by one clearing house would necessarily be accepted as good in payments of debts through any other, and thus the notes would be maintained at par over the whole country.

## SUCH ISSUES SHOULD BE LIMITED.

Such a system should include the placing of a specified limit to the issues by each clearing house in accordance with the capital and requirements of the banks of its districts. The regulation of the form of the currency and of all liabilities in connection therewith should be governed by an act of Congress. Within the limits assigned by legislation there would be full scope for the exercise of discretion by clearing houses. Experience shows that the wants of the business community are better and safer guides than any preconceived ideas of what the amount of issues should be. Banks are the best judges, not singly but collectively, and their tendency is always to restrict credits and impose limits not only on themselves but on their customers. If a maximum limit of issues were fixed by law, it is certain that the actual issues would always be far below it.

## THREE ADVANTAGES OF A CLEARING HOUSE CURRENCY.

The advantages of a redeemable currency are threefold.

### IT IS EXPANSIVE.

First, it is expansive. This point has been largely covered by what has been already said, and it only remains to notice that such a system is so adaptive that when once adjusted it would respond to the annual demands for currency at different seasons in different parts of the country, noiselessly and without friction. Movements of the crops, which now take place with much difficulty, would be provided for without disturbance. The natural operations of trade and business would be encouraged, assisted, and developed by the most potent agent civilization has yet devised, which is a well secured bank note circulation.

### IT IS RETIRED WHEN DEMAND CEASES.

But, secondly, its advantage is chiefly in the retirement of the notes when their work is done. Fixed currency is never retired except by shipping it out of the country, and it is never increased to meet a sudden demand except by shipping it back. Both of these operations are cumbersome and expensive, and no more intelligent than we should expect to find prevailing among the tribes of Africa. To attempt to supply domestic needs by importations of gold, and to dispose of our surplus by shipping it, is a crude and barbarous device, that may be likened to the Chinese method of burning villages to secure a little roast pork, that Charles Lamb tells us of. Under our present system, the importations and exportations of gold, which should pass unnoticed, shake business to its centre, and become events of national importance. A redeemable paper currency would obviate all this by supplying our domestic wants at home.

### DANGERS FROM ACCUMULATIONS.

If the amount of fixed currency is maintained at a figure large enough to enable it to perform all special services in the busy season of the year, then in the dull season, usually the summer months, it would accumulate in idleness at the money centres. Watts's couplet, —

> "Satan finds some mischief still
> For idle hands to do,"

is especially applicable to idle currency. Financial adventurers are waiting for a plethora of money to tempt idle funds with specious schemes. But an expansive currency is not exposed to this danger. When money is wanted under such a system, there is no lack of it; when it is not wanted, it is retired and there is no slack. It is the slack which is the bane of banking. No lack, no slack, is the best description of a redeemable paper currency.

### IT WOULD PREVENT PANICS.

The third benefit of a redeemable paper currency is that it would be a preventive of money panics, and the consequent evils of forced liquidations at frequent intervals. A forced liquidation is incident to any system that does not admit of expansion in case of need, just as steam boilers are liable to explode if they have no safety-valves. If all the currency of a country is fixed, that is, metal or representative of metal, no matter how much there is of it, even if the amount is greater than the dream of the most ardent silver advocate, and if the banks are conducted on the principle of a reserve of a certain percentage, a crisis of want of confidence is liable to happen at any time when a serious calamity occurs or threatens to occur. This want of confidence shows itself in a demand from creditors for currency to the extent of their credit balances, which soon depletes the banks of their reserves. A bank cannot refuse to meet this demand and maintain its solvency, for the creditors own the cash in the bank. They understand what a reserve means, and that the man who runs the quickest is the surest to get his money. On an even distribution every creditor would receive 10 per cent. of his credit balance in cash, but he wants it all in cash. *Hinc illæ lachrymæ!* By a long series of similar experiences the whole army of creditors is trained to run, and they put their acquirement into exercise on every reasonable or unreasonable provocation with a unanimity, precision, and effectiveness which are worthy of a better cause. The means of self-protection which the banks have is the collection of loans, bills receivable, and other debts. As a run comes suddenly the banks must collect suddenly, and debtors are expected to pay promptly. All debtors must therefore put their property up for sale on a market bare of cash, sell it at whatever sacrifice, and liquidate their loans. As a consequence prices decline heavily, many failures occur, and general distress follows. If the currency of an isolated country like ours is fixed and admits of no expansion, and banks keep only a reserve, these seasons of forced liquidation must come whenever a financial calamity overshadows the land. If they come every few years it is evident that the losses consequent on the sales at the great declines and the small returns during the following depressions would destroy the profits of business, weaken the financial position of the country, and largely increase the chances of subsequent failures.

#### PREVENTION OF PANICS OF THE UTMOST CONSEQUENCE.

It is therefore of the utmost importance to the solvency and welfare of the community that the banking system should confer on the banks the power to meet these occasions of lack of confidence and carry the business interests of the nation over without disaster. One of the objects of the currency system should be to reduce preventable failures to a minimum and to grant all needed facilities to legitimate business. Twelve thousand failures are too many to occur in one year in our country, and from three to five years is too short an interval between money panics.

These ends can only be accomplished by giving to banks the power to issue bank notes to the business community according to its needs, on convertible collateral, whenever a crisis or a legitimate demand occurs.

#### BULLION COMMITTEE OF 1810.

The report of the Bullion Committee of 1810 of the English House of Commons laid down the principle that "an enlarged accommodation is the true remedy for that occasional failure of confidence to which a system of paper credit is unavoidably exposed." The truth of this principle has been confirmed by every money panic in the eighty-three years which have followed its enunciation.

From the above discussion it is concluded that our country needs, first, a fixed circulation of gold and silver sufficient for the ordinary payments of its domestic and foreign exchanges, and second, a redeemable paper currency which **may expand and contract with the demands of trade.**

# XIII

## THE PHILOSOPHY OF THE HISTORY OF BANK CURRENCY IN THE UNITED STATES[1]

### BANKING OF THREE KINDS.

BANKING is of three kinds; or, it may be said, banking has passed through three stages of development. In the first it is a common-law right, in the second a charter privilege, and in the third a right free to all under general banking laws. Each kind, or stage, has its controlling characteristic. In the first, the rights of the individual, in the second, the rights of the governing power, and in the third, the rights of the people, are respectively paramount.

The second stage includes all there is in the first, with the supremacy of the State added; the third, all in the first and the second, with the supremacy of the people added.

Though in its early history there was no clear definition of what the term banking meant, it is evident, from legal decisions and commercial usages, as quoted by MacLeod in his "Theory of Credit," that its original and fundamental idea was the right and power to issue notes to circulate as money.

[1] Reprinted from the *Bankers' Magazine*, February, 1895.

## COMMON-LAW RIGHT TO ISSUE CURRENCY WITHDRAWN.

Under the well-founded plea of public policy and necessity, in the United States and in most civilized countries, the common-law right to issue currency has been taken away from individuals and unauthorized corporations, and has been left as the prerogative only of specially chartered banks and banks organized under general laws. The common-law right to engage in banking has, therefore, been limited to ordinary commercial transactions.

The necessity for the restriction of the common-law right, as it was exercised in England in 1825, and before that time, is shown by the following extract from a speech delivered by Lord Liverpool on the 17th of February of that year. He said: "The present system of law as to banks must now be altered in one way or another. It is the most absurd. By it a cobbler or a cheesemonger, without any proof of his ability to meet them, might issue his notes unrestricted by any check whatever."

In the United States the same condition of affairs existed, as is shown by the following extract from the report of the Committee on Banks made to the Senate of the State of New York, February 25, 1837. The report says : —

"The issuing of individual notes for circulation was the great practical evil which called into existence the restraining law (of 1818). The State had become literally covered with the notes of Barker's Exchange Bank, the Utica Insurance

Company, the Little Falls Aqueduct Association, and the small notes of Benjamin Rathbone, Calvin Cheeseman, and a host of unremembered individuals and corporations, tavern-keepers, glass-makers, merchants, turnpike companies, etc."

Governor Marcy, in his annual message, January 3, 1837, said : —

" The privilege of issuing a paper circulating medium cannot be given to all individuals and associations that desire to have it, without exposing the public to evils against which it is the duty of the legislature to afford ample and certain protection."

From the reports of the United States Currency Commission, it would appear that Belgium forms perhaps the only exception in this particular, and that in that country, even at the present time, the right to issue currency is not restricted, but may be enjoyed by individuals as well as by chartered institutions.

### SPECIALLY CHARTERED BANKS.

Though the common-law right to issue currency no longer exists in this country, its exercise was a necessary precursor of legalized and restricted banking, and in discussing that subject there remain but the two divisions under which it may be classified : First, specially chartered banks ; second, banks organized under free, or general, laws.

In considering the distinctions between these two classes of banks some of the fundamental questions of banking will be discussed, and their connection with the currency questions now before the public will be perceived.

This country inherited from England language, religion, social and business habits, and the common law, but only so much of the latter as was not in conflict with the fundamental principles of the Declaration of Independence.

After the Revolution there was a continuous adjustment of the inherited legislative methods and practices to bring them into accord with true republican ideas.

Our only financial model worthy of imitation was the charter of the Bank of England, and the first banks of the United States were organized, like that bank, under special charters, and were intended to be monopolies.

The opinion then prevailed in the commercial world on the other side of the Atlantic that one bank was sufficient for one nation. There were the Banks of Venice, Amsterdam, of France, England, Ireland, Scotland, and it was concluded here that there should be one Bank of North America, which was chartered in 1781, with authority to open offices in various cities at will.

But when the independence and sovereignty of the States was established, then the plan of chartering a bank for each one of the States met approval, and the Massachusetts Bank, the Bank of New York, and a bank for Maryland were chartered by the legislatures of those several States.

Soon afterward Congress gave a charter to the first Bank of the United States, with the intention of granting to it special privileges and monopolies.

The granting of bank charters speedily became a great source of dishonest revenue to members of the various state legislatures, and, as the result of disgraceful corruption, a whole brood of state banks obtained charters and were organized.

Albert Gallatin wrote in 1831: "With the exception of Mr. Girard's bank, all the banks established in the United States are joint stock companies, incorporated by law, with a fixed capital, to the extent of which only the stockholders are generally responsible."

But the lack of harmony between specially chartered banks and the principle of representative government soon made itself felt. The contest against banking monopoly was first waged over the United States Bank as its most conspicuous example.

Few contests, short of war, were of greater virulence or had a greater moulding influence on the development of republican thought than that which resulted in the overthrow of the United States Bank. General Jackson wrote that that event was necessary " to preserve the morals of the people, the freedom of the press, and the purity of the elective franchise." This fairly expresses the sentiment of the country, which resulted in the refusal to renew the second bank's charter.

The contest did not cease with that victory, nor did the opposition to bank monopolies fully triumph until the principle of free banking was established among the States.

Petitions for a free banking law began pouring into the legislature of New York during the session of 1837 and 1838. One of the memorials may be quoted as an example. It reads: "Special and exclusive powers are contrary to and inconsistent with the genius and principles of our republican institutions. Restraints should be general in their application, so that all may participate in the business of banking on equal terms." And the Secretary of the Treasury, in his annual report in the year 1838, said: "The whole monopolies of banking might, with public advantage, be entirely abolished, and this banking privilege, under proper general restraints, securities, limitations, and requirements, may be safely thrown open to all."

In obedience to the popular wish, the free banking law of New York was passed April 18, 1838, and thereby the common-law right to issue currency was restored to the people under suitable general restrictions.

So it came to pass that the system of banking in the United States, which began on the model of the historic governmental banks of Europe, with special privileges and monopolies, was forced by the genius of American institutions, as evidenced by the act of the general government, and by the act of its chief commercial State, to be free and independent.

### BANKING UNDER REPUBLICAN PRINCIPLES.

The history of banking in the United States, in accordance with republican principles, may be justly considered to commence with the destruction of the United States Bank by General Jackson and with the adoption by New York of the principle of free banking. James De Peyster Ogden wrote in 1840: "The former commercial representative in Congress from this city (New York) considered our free banking law as equal to a second Declaration of Independence."

This was the beginning of a change in the banking system of the United States, which became universal by the passage, twenty-five years later, of the National Banking Act.

### STATE BANKING SYSTEMS IN 1863.

To avail ourselves of the wisdom and experience which was acquired by the country, and to learn what progress was made among the various States toward the adoption of general banking laws during the twenty-five years from 1838 to 1863, it is necessary to investigate the condition of state banking laws at the close of that quarter century, when in 1863 Congress took the subject of banking out of the hands of the state legislatures, largely as regards general banking and totally as regards the currency.

The development of state systems was arrested

by the national system, which was founded upon them. To understand the national system a knowledge of the state systems is necessary.

As our inquiry relates to state laws prior to 1863, we must exclude from our investigations the States which have been formed and have come into being since the establishment of the national banking system. As Congress had taxed state-bank currency out of existence, no provision for it and little attention to the subject of banking could be expected from that body.

The younger members of the family of States who have come to maturity too lately to participate in the currency discussions of from thirty to sixty years ago are: Colorado, Idaho, Nebraska, North Dakota, Montana, South Dakota, Utah, Washington, West Virginia, and Wyoming, ten in all.

In the remaining States, an examination shows that in 1863 banking systems, carefully elaborated and operating largely to the satisfaction of the people, were in operation, with four exceptions, the States of California, Oregon, Texas, and Nevada. In these four States, the remnant of a larger number which originally had the same provisions, banking and issues of circulating notes were forbidden. This was due, no doubt, to distrust of local banks, a preference for gold, the distance of these States from commercial centres, and, in the case of Nevada, perhaps, to a desire to relegate the control of banking entirely to the national government.

By separating the ten new States and the four States which have set themselves against banking and bank circulations, we have remaining the States whose legislatures had been compelled to discuss banking methods and the issue of a circulating medium as a practical question, and to pass laws regulating the subject.

### STATES GRANTING SPECIAL CHARTERS.

From these remaining States we may learn much regarding the condition and growth of American banking. They may be classified on two lines: First, the States which, before 1863, had not gone beyond the second stage of the development of banking, in which it is held to be a privilege to be enjoyed under a special charter, to be granted by special legislative act. Second, the States which, before 1863, had reached the third stage of development, in which banking is held to be " a privilege which, under proper restraints, securities, limitations, and requirements, may be safely thrown open to all."

The States of the first class were: Alabama, Arkansas, Delaware, Florida, Kentucky, Maine, Maryland, Mississippi, Missouri, New Hampshire, North Carolina, Rhode Island, South Carolina, Tennessee, and Virginia, fifteen States in all.

Several of these States have adopted new constitutions and general laws since 1863, but from the banking sections reference to a currency is generally omitted.

## STATES WITH GENERAL BANKING LAWS.

The States which have adopted free or general banking laws, either exclusively by a constitutional provision, or coördinately with chartered banks or a system of state banks with branches, by legislative enactment, are as follows, the dates being of the adoption of a constitutional provision or of the enactment of a general law: New York, April 18, 1838; Georgia, December 26, 1838; Ohio, 1845; Michigan, 1850; New Jersey, 1850; Indiana, 1851; Vermont, 1851; Massachusetts, 1851; Connecticut, 1852; Louisiana, 1855; Wisconsin, 1855; Iowa, 1857; Minnesota, 1857–58; Kansas, 1859; Pennsylvania, 1861; Illinois, 1870, — in all, sixteen States.

In some of these States the two systems existed side by side, and the laws remained on the statute-books under which special charters were granted. This gave banking capital a choice under which system to organize, and the choice was made of the system which gave the greatest freedom, or from which the greatest profit could be derived. The movement for general banking was not strong enough in all these States to make it exclusive, but whenever a general law was passed it was an approval of the principle involved and a recognition that this was the coming system.

## STATE BANKS WITH BRANCHES.

In other of these States, Ohio, Indiana, and Iowa, good systems of state banks, with branches, were organized, under general laws, with the principle of mutual responsibility for circulation, in the place of the security required by the free banking law. These state banks were deservedly popular and successful, and form the best models we have in this country for banks of their class. The details of their organization will be referred to hereafter.

### SPECIAL CHARTERS AND GENERAL LAWS COMPARED.

We have now divided the remaining States into two classes, from which we may clearly see the position of public opinion in the legislatures and among the people, from Kansas eastward, in 1863, on the question of the organization of banks by special charters or under free or general banking laws. On the one hand we have the exclusively charter States, which represent the conservative element, unchanged since colonial times, and on the other the progressive element, which, under the impetus of General Jackson's victory over the United States Bank, had carried into execution the proposition for free banking laws.

This classification is not fanciful or merely verbal, and the processes are not like two roads which converge at a common point, so that it is immaterial which road one journeys over, since a bank is the result.

The two systems are diametrically opposed to each other.

Free banking under general laws is a necessary

outgrowth of a republican form of government, and is in harmony with its institutions, and is comparatively, if not entirely, unknown outside of the United States. The short experience in 1850 of Canada with a law framed after that of New York shows that free banking is a plant which does not grow on monarchical soil, even though the government is of the most modern and enlightened type.

Banking under special charters is based on the monarchical principle of the predominant position of the government and the granting of favors to favorites, and is the rule among foreign nations.

The people of the States whose laws provide for granting only special charters to banks had never been completely disenthralled from colonial and aristocratic sentiments, manner of life, and modes of legal procedure. Their history and unchanged traditions had perpetuated among them a liking for special legislative privileges and special charters. This tendency runs through all their political principles, and it asserted itself, as a matter of course, in the system of banking they preferred.

DEVELOPMENT OF BANKING UNDER GENERAL LAWS.

It is interesting to note the progress of the idea of banking under general laws. During twelve years but two States followed the lead of New York. In spite of the failure of many of her banks in that time, and in spite of the shrinkage in value of the bonds lodged as security for currency, the States recognized that a secured currency was the only safe principle for a general law which was to provide for banks in large and small cities alike. The chronological order of the adoption of the principle by the sixteen States shows a natural and healthy spread of a system which, as it was tried and understood year after year, obtained increasing favor. It would indicate that if the National Banking Law had not been established in 1863 the country might have had, in process of time, excellent state banking systems under general laws universally adopted.

### DEVELOPMENT OF THE TWO SYSTEMS.

The record shows us that, previous to the enactment of the national law, the busy commercial North readily adopted general banking laws with their restrictions and guarantees, while the pastoral South, with its traditions, naturally preferred to keep unchanged its system of special privileges granted by the State to the favored few.

The two systems spread in the line of the development of their adjacent territory, separated by the physical boundaries of the Alleghanies. New York and Ohio gave the keynote to the North, and Maryland and Virginia to the South. They occupied all the available territory, and then it happened that, during the war, owing to the exigencies of the government, both were superseded by a new system, the National Banking Act, which is a general law, and thereby general banking became the law of the land.

## CHARACTERISTICS OF CHARTERED BANKS.

Besides the relation of special and general banking laws to republican institutions, there are other points in which they are diametrically opposed.

It seems to follow universally that when banks are specially chartered, special acquaintance with the incorporators and special confidence in their management is inferred, and these special circumstances make it seem unnecessary to require more than formal guarantees for the protection of depositors or note-holders. To grant a special privilege to a set of individuals for their own benefit, and then to demand guarantees that these privileges will be used for the benefit of others, is a contradiction in terms. This characteristic is to be noticed in all special banking legislation. This special connection binds the government to the bank, and makes it in a measure responsible for its good conduct. Consequently, small individual chartered banks in the smaller towns are an anomaly. Chartered banks should be so large in capital and business as to have a commanding credit far and wide outside of the State granting the charter.

But with general banking laws this is not so. These laws were first called "free," but that word has since been changed to "general," because the provisions of the laws were so carefully and minutely drawn that the word "free" seemed a misnomer. General banking laws require publicity, impose restrictions, and demand guarantees in the same measure that special charters omit these requirements.

### SECURED AND UNSECURED CURRENCY.

In no particular is the difference between banks organized under special and general laws more clearly and characteristically seen than in the modes of issuing currency. In the laws of all the States I have found no instance in which a specially chartered bank, or a state bank with branches, is required to make a deposit of United States or state bonds, or give other security equal in amount to the notes issued. Nor have I found a general law of any State which does not require a deposit with a state officer of collateral security at least to the full amount of the notes issued.

### GENERAL LAWS REQUIRE A SECURED CURRENCY.

This makes the broadest possible distinction between the banks of these two classes. A general law makes the provision, so simple of comprehension as to form the best basis for confidence and credit, that a deposit of bonds shall be made with a duly appointed state officer, equal in value and amount to the currency to be issued.

### SPECIAL CHARTERS FAVOR AN UNSECURED CURRENCY.

Special charters provide a number of ways by which this lack of security is made up. Some of these methods are weak and defective, and others, in a rising grade, approach nearly to a perfect security. They are in part: First, limiting the amount of the notes to be issued to a percentage of the capital of the bank. Second, giving an officer of the State power to order an examination of the bank's affairs, which is extremely pastoral. Third, requiring reports to be rendered annually, semi-annually, or quarterly. Fourth, requiring a deposit with a central bank of redemption, called the Suffolk banking system. Fifth, requiring a safety fund of a few per cent. to be deposited with the State. Sixth, forbidding the bank to increase its loans while the amount in the safety fund is below the required percentage. Seventh, requiring the bank to keep on hand in gold and silver coin $12\frac{1}{2}$, 25, or 30 per cent. of its outstanding notes. Eighth, requiring the State, and all counties in the State, to receive the notes in payment of taxes. Ninth, requiring the several branches of a state bank to receive each other's notes at par for all debts due each. Tenth, making the various branches mutually responsible for each other's notes, and, in case of failure, the solvent banks to pay contributions *pro rata* to redeem them in cash. Eleventh, giving the note-holders a preference over all the other creditors of a bank, and, in case of failure, all the assets of the bank to be turned over to a state officer for that purpose. Twelfth, forbidding the banks ever to suspend payment in gold on their notes. Thirteenth, that each and every bank shall mutually be responsible for all the debts, notes, and engagements of each other.

These provisions are to be found scattered among state laws in force in 1863, under which special charters were granted, or state banks with branches were organized. The most stringent laws have been found to work well and to be accompanied by the fewest failures.

## CAN AN UNSECURED CURRENCY BE MADE GOOD.

If it were desired to construct a good system of banking out of these provisions, with an unsecured currency, it could be made by including device numbered seventh, that each bank shall keep 30 per cent. of its outstanding notes in gold in its vaults at all times; ninth, the provision found in the laws of Kentucky and other States, that the notes of the "mother bank" and of each branch shall be current in every other; tenth, the provision found in the laws of Iowa and other States, that solvent branches of the state bank must contribute *pro rata* to the fund for the redemption of the notes of failed banks; eleventh, giving note-holders a preference over other creditors of a bank; and, thirteenth, the Indiana provision, which, as stated in the law, reads that "each and every branch of the Bank of the State of Indiana shall mutually be responsible for all the debts, notes, and engagements of each other."

It cannot be said that such a system is impossible or impracticable, for state banks with branches were organized and flourished under these regulations; for instance, in Ohio, Indiana, Iowa, Missouri, and Kentucky, before the National Banking Law went into operation.

#### HOYT SHERMAN ON IOWA STATE BANK.

Concerning the Iowa State Bank, Hoyt Sherman, a veteran banker, and brother of the General and of Senator Sherman, said before the Iowa State Bankers' Association in 1894: "From the start these branches secured the complete confidence of the communities where located, and their circulation was welcomed and sought after by all classes as an equivalent to gold. During the course of their business history a few of the branches at different times made mistakes in their investments, or temporarily mismanaged funds in their hands. These events worked no injury to their customers or the public, and in fact were not known outside of bank circles until long after they were passed and the dangers overcome. The cool, dispassioned, unprejudiced judgment of the other branches enables them to see the danger at once, and apply the remedy in time to protect their crippled brother, as well as to avoid on their part a contingent liability. They became a strong illustration of the principle of fellowship in business, underlying the state bank system."

Many would prefer a system of secured currency, without mutual responsibility and other safeguards, to an unsecured currency with their safeguards. But to give the country an unsecured currency, without the strongest guarantees, is to take a step backward and to unite the weakest halves of the special charter and general law system; and the result would be one too weak to hold together.

No currency not secured by deposit of ample collaterals should be proposed or adopted unless it is surrounded by the safeguards which experience has shown to be effective.

### CLEARING HOUSE CERTIFICATES.

In 1857, 1860, and 1861, and at various times since the establishment of the national banking system, and perhaps in large measure necessitated by the inelasticity both of the state and national systems, the country has become acquainted with " a currency between banks " in the form of clearing house certificates. These show to us the features of a currency which the most conservative of our banks, at the present time, consider the best for themselves.

### PROVISIONS FOR THEIR SECURITY.

These features are, first, that the clearing house currency is secured by pledge of commercial assets in the hands of a committee acting as trustee for the note-holders.

This provision is derived from the New York state law.

Second, the associated banks agree to take the notes in settlement of all claims against any of their number. This is similar to the provisions of the law of Kentucky and other States.

Third, if any loss occurs from the insufficiency of the collateral, or the insolvency of the banks to whom the certificates are issued, it is to be apportioned *pro rata* among the associated banks. This is in accordance with the laws of Iowa and other States.

Fourth, the banks thereby agree to stand by each other with all the cash in their control, and this is, in effect, the principle of the Indiana law.

CLEARING HOUSE CURRENCY A COMBINATION OF SPECIAL AND GENERAL LAWS.

This clearing house system is a combination of the strongest features of both the special and general laws as regards the issue of currency. It is evident that by dividing all banks in the country into clearing house districts and incorporating clearing houses under United States laws, it would be no difficult matter to extend it over the whole nation, and thereby obtain a currency good at every clearing house, the features of which have been tested by experience for fifty years and found good.[1]

A system is not complete which incorporates banks and leaves clearing houses to be organized under local laws. The national law should provide for the incorporation of clearing houses, so that their action shall be uniform. To protect the association in its guarantees, power should be given it to declare any bank insolvent which did not make its collateral satisfactory on demand, and it should be a preferred creditor until the notes issued were paid.

[1] This suggestion is elaborated more fully in chapters xi. and xii. entitled "The Completion of the National Banking System" and "Fixed and Redeemable Currency." See pp. 152, 159.

The watchfulness over the business methods and practices of associated banks, which lies at the basis of such a system, would be a great protection to the community. A bankers' association would then mean more than pleasant social intercourse. Its rules and regulations would then have the full effect of laws, with power to enforce them. The clearing house then would take the position which the board of directors of a state bank occupied toward the branches, who transacted no business except with them.

The fundamental distinction between the special and general state banking laws, then, is found in the methods adopted for the issue of currency.

### THE RISE OF THE PRINCIPLE OF A SECURED CURRENCY.

The issue of a secured currency marks the rise of a new principle in banking, and it is therefore well to endeavor to trace it to its source.

This new principle, as has been said, took shape in this country first in the New York law of 1838. It was incorporated also in the charter of the Bank of England in 1844, six years subsequently to the enactment of the New York law. By a reference to the public discussions of that time in England, it would appear that the proposal for a secured currency was made at least as early as 1825, and perhaps earlier. Lord Liverpool declared, in 1825, "that a system (of banking) was wanted which would exclude the possibility of discredit and bankruptcy, by preventing every individual or association from issuing notes without an adequate guarantee."

In 1826 Henry Drummond wrote: " It is further proposed that all issuers of notes should deposit a security for the notes which they issue."

Joplin, in his "Essay on Banking" (1827), wrote: " Two chief plans for the protection of the public against improper banking are, first, to compel bankers to register their property, and, secondly, to give security for their notes in circulation."

INFLUENCE OF WEBSTER'S OPINION.

Lord Overstone wrote in a pamphlet, issued in 1840: " The two things, the management of a paper currency and the management of banking deposits, cannot be blended together in one system and treated as subject to the same laws and to be governed by the same principles." He quoted with approval from Webster's speech of March 12, 1838, on the Sub-Treasury Bill, where he expressed the belief that " *a national bank might be established with more regard to its functions of regulating currency than to its function of discount.*" This quotation he used with impressive effect, and in a manner most complimentary to Webster, in advocating the separation of those functions in the Bank of England.

James De Peyster Ogden (New York, 1840) writes: " An opinion prevails in England that there should be a bank of issue distinct from a bank of discount, and Mr. Loyd (afterwards Lord Overstone), in his late pamphlet, favors the idea, but suggests no plan." "We should not have thought it necessary to allude to this proposed experiment, had we not found that an idea had been occasionally expressed in favor of the feasibility of some principle of the kind in this country." He then proceeds to argue against the New York law. So it would appear that the suggestion of a secured currency came to New York from England, where it first arose after the banking troubles which culminated in 1825, and it was carried into effect both in New York and in London, as a sequence of the panic of 1837. This great principle was therefore the joint product of the currency debates in England and America, and its object was, as Lord Liverpool said, "to exclude the possibility of discredit and bankruptcy."

### A SECURED CURRENCY THOUGHT TO BE A PANACEA.

In the history of every panic, and the remark is true of every form of public calamity, it is to be noticed that, after its first effects have passed away, the minds of legislators and business men have been occupied with the framing of devices intended to prevent a recurrence of similar troubles.

The separation of the banking department from the department of issue and the securing of the circulation of the Bank of England was the fruit of the troubles which culminated in the panic of 1837.

It was then fondly hoped that the secret had been discovered by which future panics might be avoided. No panic of equal extent and violence to that of 1837 has since visited the commercial world, and that fact has no doubt been due in large measure to the introduction and adoption of the principle of a secured currency and the accumulation of a great mass of gold which it necessitates. That panics have since occurred should lead, not to the abandonment of the principle, but to its still further adjustment, so that it may accomplish all that has been hoped from it.

PEEL'S LAW OF EQUILIBRIUM NOT A NECESSARY PART OF SEPARATION.

The " fantastic theory," as MacLeod calls it, for the regulation of the currency by the " law of equilibrium," contained in Peel's act, which has often been condemned as contrary to the principles of the Bullion Report of 1810, and of common sense, need not be referred to. The primary object of the New York law of 1838, and of the bank charter of 1844, was the same; that is, to make a separation between the two functions of a bank, general banking and the issue of currency, and to provide security for the latter.

REASONS FOR SEPARATION OF ISSUE DEPARTMENT IN BANK OF ENGLAND.

One of the reasons for this separation was stated by Lord Overstone to be the liability to the abuse of the power of issue. Experience has shown that this is inevitable; that the facility of issuing currency is fatal, the temptation to make money by the use of legal privileges to their fullest extent overcomes prudence and conservatism. It is too great a temptation for the average bank officer to resist, and it is necessary to guard against the dangers which result therefrom by provisions made part of the banking law. The restraints of wisdom, experience, public opinion, prudence, and self-interest are not enough. As Washington said, "Influence is not government." So, in the case of banks, the principle must be stated in the law if we would have it govern.

Colonel Torrens, who with S. J. Loyd (afterwards Lord Overstone) shares the credit of the change in the charter of the Bank of England by which the issue department was separated from the banking, and the currency was secured by gold and government bonds, wrote in defense of Sir Robert Peel's bill that Parliament had "committed a mistake in delegating to the directors of the Bank of England the important functions of securing the convertibility of the currency;" and he gives instances prior to 1844 when they abused that power, which was taken away from them by Peel's act. In the present day we can do no more than reëcho the words of Colonel Torrens, "It would be a mistake for Congress to give to the directors of the banks of the United States the liberty of issuing currency and of holding the security themselves."

## EXPLOSIVE CHARACTER OF AN UNSECURED CURRENCY.

But the most serious objection to the demand that the banks shall have this liberty is in the fact that it would imperil the financial situation by increasing the obligations of banks in their most "explosive" form. The distinction between a demand from depositors and from note-holders is very clear. Depositors do a current business with a bank and are bound to it by favors past, present, and prospective. Note-holders have no such relations, and when the credit of a bank is blown upon they send in its notes for payment as rapidly as they can be gathered. If there is no trustee to take care of the interests of the note-holder, he must act for himself. This he does in short order, by presenting the notes for redemption. Not one note, but all may be expected to be presented. One run starts another, and there can be no mutual support. Such a currency is deceptive. It masquerades as true and honest money until the mask falls, when it is seen to be only a bank's debt of uncertain and unknown value.

The more there is of this kind of currency, the greater the disaster when a panic overtakes a community. It contracts in a panic with fearful velocity. If it is issued again it will be returned for payment the next day. It affords no relief in time of trouble; but, on the contrary, is the greatest source of bankruptcy among banks which shortsighted and inexcusable folly has yet devised.

In quiet waters sometimes unseaworthy boats win races from their stouter competitors. So, in times of undisturbed tranquillity, a chartered bank, in being able to issue its currency directly to borrowers, has an advantage over a bank that must first buy bonds or make some other arrangement to get currency. But this defect is remedied to a great degree if commercial assets may be pledged. The advantage, then, which a chartered bank has is slight, for both would first loan their own resources, and when the opportunity or necessity came for the issuing and loaning of currency, the routine of making an application to a clearing house would not present an appreciable difficulty, while the great point of security for the currency issued, in which the public has everything at stake, would be gained.

### SECURED CURRENCY COMMANDS CONFIDENCE.

How different from an unsecured currency is one which is secured by the pledge of convertible assets, be they commercial or government securities, in the hands of a responsible trustee, a treasurer of a State or of the United States, or a committee of a clearing house association, who holds the security for the benefit of the note-holder. There is no mask to fall from it. Confidence in it rests not on the bank issuing the notes, but on the security pledged, which is of well-known character, or has been approved by competent persons who are interested in protecting themselves against a contingent loss, and on the character of the trustee.

In no panic has the redemption of national bank notes been a source of trouble to the bank issuing them. On the contrary, all eyes are turned at such times in the direction of additional issues of bank notes as a measure of relief. But commercial banks do not, and should not, own government bonds to any extent, and their commercial assets are not receivable as security for currency. Consequently, the legal mode, under the present law, in which the currency might be made elastic, is closed to the banks in their time of greatest need. It was for this reason that the banks of New York have at various times turned to the only way by which a substitute for currency could be procured, and in the issue of clearing house certificates they provided themselves with an emergency currency which, though limited in use, imperfect in form, and extra-legal in character, brought widespread and great relief to the community. This action by the banks of New York, from 1857 to 1893, illustrates the principle that a currency, to be a relief to the business community, must be issued on application by the banks, and on a pledge of security of approved character with a trustee of acknowledged standing before the nation.

The vital advantage nowadays in a bank currency is to provide a safety valve to avoid explosions. The universal use of checks and the rapidity of communication by railroad, mail, and telegraph, make currency of less importance in daily business, except as change. The words of the Bullion Report of 1810 may be used to describe the chief service of a bank currency, which is to afford the true remedy for that occasional failure of confidence to which our system of paper credit is unavoidably exposed.

## DEDUCTIONS.

The deductions made from this discussion of the history of the currency are : —

First. Issues of currency by a bank which holds the security thereto in its own hands, of which the specially chartered bank is the model, add to its burdens and obligations. The inducement to these issues are, that they are a source of profit to the issuer and of temporary accommodation to the borrower. In time of panic such issues have a disastrous effect in rapidly depleting the cash reserves of the bank, and are a mockery and embarrassment. Customers are compelled by this note contraction to incur unnecessary losses for the protection of the bank. The operation of such a currency is, first, to stimulate business to an unhealthy activity by means of an increased note circulation, and then to wreck it by a forced liquidation on a market bare of purchasers to provide the bank with funds to pay its notes.

Second. Issues of currency on specific pledge of approved convertible collateral security, such as government bonds or commercial assets, to a bank of which one organized under a general law is the model, add to its cash resources, and are a support and defense to the commercial world in time of panic. They enable the bank to accommodate its customers when they are most in need, and thus cause the machinery of business to move on smoothly and without disturbance.

In such a system may be combined the best features of special and general laws, and from that combination may be secured a defense against monetary panics, which will, as J. R. McCulloch[1] says, " mitigate, if not entirely obviate," their evil results.

[1] In his edition (1849) of Adam Smith, p. 502.

# APPENDIX

## STATEMENTS OF THE VIEWS OF VARIOUS WRITERS REFERRED TO IN THE PREFACE

PLAN OF CHARLES PARSONS, OF ST. LOUIS.

CHARLES PARSONS, President of the State Bank of St. Louis, and an Ex-President of the American Bankers' Association, seeing the article in the "Bankers' Magazine" on "The Completion of the National Banking System," sent me under date of October 10, 1893, a copy "of a proposition," he writes, "which I sent Mr. Carlisle on August 1st last, and which I drew up in 1884. Of course this plan would have to be put in legal shape for a bill to put before Congress." Mr. Parsons's national prominence as a banker gives the greatest weight to his suggestion, and I copy the plan in its entirety.

*A Plan for a United States Clearing House Currency for Emergencies.*

I propose that Congress pass a law for the issue of from seventy-five to one hundred million of dollars of currency notes solely for use during times of financial panic.

These notes shall be printed and prepared for use under direction of the United States Treasury Department; shall be countersigned by the Treasurer and registered by the Register.

They shall be delivered to the various clearing houses of the country in such proportions as the importance of the place in business warrants, none, however, to be delivered to any place having less than $5,000,000 of banking capital represented in its clearing house.

A committee of five shall be appointed to consider applications for loans of this currency by banks in each clearing house, and the Bank Examiner for the district, or some person well acquainted with the value of securities and the business men of the city, shall be appointed by the Secretary of the Treasury, and shall be an additional member of said committee.

This committee shall receive from applying banks good bills receivable maturing and not having more than four months to run, or good interest-paying bonds of States, counties, and cities of the United States, or first mortgage bonds of dividend-paying railroads, and shall issue to such banks, in reasonable amounts as the committee deems wise, $750 for each $1,000 of security thus deposited; for which the borrowing bank shall execute and deliver its collateral bill payable, with pledge, which shall become due not more than four months from date of issue at farthest, and draw interest at six per cent. per annum. The committee may reduce the time the bill payable has to run in its discretion or to suit the borrowing bank.

Before any currency shall be delivered to any clearing house, its members shall by a unanimous vote agree to become responsible for the ultimate redemption. If a special law is required to authorize such guaranty, it shall become a part of this bill.

The banks securing the currency from the committees shall also agree to redeem it as it is presented at their duly named agency in the city of New York, and a failure to redeem it shall cause the bill payable given for it to become due and payable at once, and the issuing committee shall be authorized to sell the pledged securities and redeem said currency without any delay.

The notes of which this currency is to be composed shall be of various denominations, from five to twenty dollars, and are to be considered as emergency notes, and the necessity and time of their issue shall be fixed by the President of the United States whenever he deems there is an emergency in which the public interests and the financial condition of the country require it ; and notice shall be publicly given by him when he so considers the necessity to exist.

Within six months from the date on which the President shall order the issue of this currency to the clearing houses of the country, each clearing house shall return said currency taken by it to the Treasurer of the United States, and for and in place of any such notes as it may not be able to thus return (by reason of being in circulation), gold or United States legal tender money may be paid over, which shall be held by the government for the redemption of such unreturned notes.

The interest secured from the loans made under this law shall be divided as follows : —

First. The expense of preparing the currency and its transmission to the various clearing houses shall be remitted to the United States Treasurer on receipt by the various clearing houses, in proportion as they have received of the currency.

Second. One fourth ($\frac{1}{4}$) of the remainder shall be paid to the United States Treasurer to be by him turned into the treasury, and the remainder shall belong to the clearing houses, to be divided by them among the banks in proportion to the value represented by each (counting capital and accumulated surplus) as guarantors of the loans made.

The final settlement of interest shall be made and balance due the government paid over within six months from the date of the President's order for issue of the currency.

The general management of the issue of the currency might be under the same department of the treasury as that of the national banks. The currency is to be signed by the president and manager of each clearing house issuing it.

EXPLANATION.

The object of this currency is to provide, when, as in 1857 and 1873 and now, the people become unduly excited and distrustful, being disposed to withdraw money from solvent banks, thus curtailing the capacity of such institutions to accommodate the public, imperiling the existence of solvent and well managed banks, producing also unreasonable declines in the values of various reliable and safe bonds and stocks, closing up factories, throwing out of occupation worthy and industrious citizens, ending in a wild and senseless scramble for money, that the emergency currency shall be forthcoming to supply the place of that withdrawn by a frightened public from the banks.

This currency bears on its face not a guaranty of the government, but has its stamp and register, like the national bank note, to show that it is under its care and watch. It would be issued against a genuine value to solvent parties, and will be secured, first, by the guaranty of each clearing house, and, secondly, by the banks receiving it, with their best securities behind it.

I limit the issue to towns having $5,000,000 bank capital, as I wish to have the character of the currency above dispute, so that it will circulate freely and have every element of safety to gain public confidence.

I provide for its redemption within six months, because otherwise it would not be an emergency currency, but likely to be permanent, and thus we would lose this avenue of relief in times of public danger such as now exists.

This plan I suggested in 1884, but as the panic was then short and comparably feeble, did not put it before the public. I now submit it as perhaps affording a means of great benefit.

CHARLES PARSONS.

St. Louis, Mo., August 1, 1893.

In order to facilitate the success of this plan, I further recommend the passage of a bill by Congress authorizing the issuing of charters to the various clearing houses in the country, providing for the receipt by them of such currency as is spoken of herein, and its signature and issue to the various banks in each of them within limits named.

CHARLES PARSONS.

St. Louis, Mo., November 13, 1897.

Since Mr. Parsons now adopts the incorporation of clearing houses under a federal law, there remains only the recognition of state boundaries, so as to give a clearing house of issue to each State, the acceptance of the clearing house currency by all clearing houses, and several minor provisions, as the reason for the preparation of another scheme. But these additions and the formulation of the whole in a workable bill, and the fortification of the plan by an appeal to history, the experience of other countries, and to the principles of political economy, seemed called for to secure a full understanding of the subject, and that work has been attempted in this volume. Mr. Parsons writes: "So far as my opinion of it goes, this new currency plan will finally dispense with United States treasury notes."

PLAN OF EDWARD ATKINSON, OF BOSTON.

After the introduction of my bill in Congress, I learned that Mr. Edward Atkinson had proposed a similar idea, and at my request he kindly sent me a copy of an address on Finance and Banking, delivered at the dinner of the Boston Boot and Shoe Club, December 17, 1890.

In that address he gives the rough draft of an act which he believed would establish confidence and credit. I quote as follows: —

I think my plan will be most easily comprehended by reciting the main provisions of this act.

An act authorizing national banks to issue secured notes, which may serve as a circulating medium, in addition to the bank notes, now authorized and now secured by the deposits of United States bonds.

Be it enacted that any    banks having an aggregate capital of $    in each of the districts bounded and described as follows, to wit: (No. 1, 2, 3, etc., by boundaries) of which the following cities may be held to be the respective centres (No. 1, 2, 3, etc.), may organize a clearing house in each of the said cities respectively, for the following purposes and with the following lawful powers in addition to the customary powers usually conferred upon a clearing house association by the banks which now belong to such associations which are not covered by or made a part of this act.

After prescribing the manner of organizing such clearing houses, designating the officers and defining their respective duties, the lawful powers conferred might be substantially in the following form : —

I. Any national bank in each of said districts may place in the charge of the finance committee of said clearing house, securities in which no more than    per cent. of the capital of said bank may be invested ; which securities shall be subject to change or to addition thereto upon the demand of the finance committee of said clearing house, whenever any of said securities shall become unsatisfactory to them. Such securities shall also be subject to be changed from time to time, with the assent of the finance committee of the clearing house, according to the convenience or necessity of the business of the depositing bank.

II. Upon the deposit of such securities, satisfactory in amount and quality to the finance committee of said clearing house, this fact shall be certified to the executive officers of the clearing house; such officers shall then issue clearing house certificates printed in the form of bank notes, in sums of not less than one dollar or more than    dollars. On the back of said certificates there shall be a statement that the bank named in such certificate has deposited securities in amount and quality satisfactory to the clearing house, valued at 25 per cent. in excess of the amount of the certificates of which this certificate number    constitutes one of series number    This certificate is issued subject to an agreement by said bank to maintain the amount of securities held by the clearing house, so that the sum of said securities in the estimation of the committee shall at no time be less than 25 per cent. in excess of the amount of certificates issued thereon. In consideration of which deposit of securities, and for other good and valuable considerations, the said clearing house hereby guarantees the payment or redemption of this note on demand in lawful money by said bank. In default of such payment, said clearing house will promptly redeem this note at par in lawful money, and may then sell the securities deposited with it to recover the amount due. In witness of which obligation the said clearing house binds itself by its seal and its obligation thereto affixed. (The method of executing the obligation left for further consideration. Provision to be made for the certificates of each clearing house district to be printed in such different colors or combinations that the sorting may be facilitated. Provision also to be made to make each clearing house the primary place of redemption, so that the work of redemption may be very simple.)

III. Upon the reverse side of the note on which this obligation of the clearing house shall have been executed, the bank to which these certificates shall have been issued shall cause to be printed or inscribed in the usual manner its obligation to pay in lawful money on demand the specific sum, one     dollars, as the case may be, corresponding to the sum named in the certificate given by the clearing house, which obligation shall be executed in due form, and signed by the president and cashier of said bank.

Section No. IV. may be framed so as to relieve these notes from the tax on circulation, to which any notes issued by state banks are now subject.

Subsequent sections may be framed so as to provide for subjecting this branch of the business of the national banks and also the clearing houses authorized to do this business, to examination under the direction of the Comptroller of the national banks, of the same kind and in the same manner as that to which all national banks are now subject in respect to the business which they are now authorized to transact.

Also sections may be framed prescribing the manner of printing the clearing house obligations and notes for registry under the supervision of the Comptroller.

I submit that in this way absolute security may be imparted to the note circulation, prompt redemption may be assured, stability will be imparted to all credit which is based on adequate capital and character, while at the same time no jealousy will be excited such as would be aroused by renewing a proposal for a great national bank. Each clearing house would be a check upon the next so that not one could exist which was not safely administered, while in the end the system would lead to the authorization and establishment of branches of the banks in the smaller towns where the business would not warrant a separate bank, thus incorporating in our own system the most beneficent feature of the Scotch method.

Next Saturday's Bradstreet will contain the rough draft of the Act, which is now being dealt with by some of my friends, who are perhaps more competent than I am in this branch of the work, with a view to perfecting it.

If Mr. Atkinson's plan had recognized state boundaries and had provided that notes issued by one clearing house should be accepted by all others throughout the nation, thus maintaining them at par, and had contained a few other practical features, it would have accomplished all the objects desired. But his proposal lacked these essential provisions for a universal system, and he seems never to have put it into the shape of a bill that he was willing to have introduced in Congress. He consulted some friends, forgetting the axiom that a council of war never fights. As he has not advocated the idea in recent years, it must be presumed that his interest in the plan for some reason has not been sustained.

The criticism on Mr. Atkinson's plan from bankers in interior cities, like Saint Paul and Minneapolis, was that clearing house currency issued and redeemed as provided in his bill would be the means of depleting the reserves of country banks and would therefore be as dangerous as paying out legal money directly. Consequently his scheme was not thought to propose any measure of relief in a money pressure. This objection, which is fatal, would not hold if the notes were accepted by all clearing houses at par, and redemption effected by them.

## SUGGESTIONS OF D. G. AMBLER, OF JACKSONVILLE, FLORIDA.

Another proposition of somewhat the same character was made by Mr. D. G. Ambler, President of the National Bank of the State of Florida, Jacksonville, Florida, in a paper submitted by him at the meeting of the American Bankers' Asociation held in Chicago, in 1893. It is as follows : —

1st. Let Congress authorize national banks to form associations with themselves and other banks for clearing house and other purposes as hereinafter provided for.

2d. Authorize such associations as have an aggregate capital and surplus of $50,000,000 to issue circulation from time to time, by and with the assent of the Secretary of the Treasury and the Comptroller of the Currency.

3d. To loan this circulation to its members (and perhaps to others) on the same security as they now loan certificates, viz. : only 75 per cent. of the value of the security.

4th. For the first 15 per cent. of an amount equal to the aggregate capital and surplus of the banks in the association the rate of interest is to be 6 per cent.

The next 15 per cent. to be 7 per cent., and so on up.

And any bank not repaying its loan in six months shall pay the maximum rate imposed on any, and that to be raised 1 per cent. each month till paid.

5th. The interest thus paid for these loans, less expenses of the association, is to be deposited in the Treasury of the United States, to the credit of the association, for future emergencies.

6th. As the loans are paid, the same are to be paid into the United States Treasury for the payment of the circulation heretofore provided for.

7th. The circulation shall be redeemed at any time by the clearing house, and is a legal tender to any member thereof. Shall also be payable at the nearest sub-treasury.

8th. The association shall keep as a redemption fund at

all times in the nearest sub-treasury a sum of legal tender money equal to 5 per cent. of the circulation outstanding, less the amount that may have been deposited to redeem the same.

We thus have a system that legalizes the clearing house association and makes it regular and correct for any bank to ask for help for its customers. This system also being under control of the treasury and currency department of the government.

We have a circulation guaranteed by associations of such magnitude as to make the circulation good beyond doubt. For instance, the New York Clearing House to-day represents a capital and surplus equal to about double the capital of the Bank of England. Further, we have as security $100 of securities carefully scrutinized by the association for every $75 of circulation issued. We make such a rate of interest as insures the retirement of the loans, and consequently the circulation, or its equivalent, in six months or thereabouts, and thus prevent permanent inflation. The rates of interest prevent the banks making use of it save in an emergency, but the certainty that the relief can be had will prevent panic by insuring public confidence. If it is said that the banks would not go into a system with no profits to them, I say they have done it repeatedly. Witness the clearing house certificate, with no profit or hope of profit to the bank.

This scheme, while fragmentary, shows that the plan of incorporating clearing houses would have its advocates in the South, as in other parts of the country.

### THE LATE ADOLPH LADENBURG'S ARTICLE IN THE "FORUM," JANUARY, 1896.

One of the most able and interesting discussions of this subject was by the late Adolph Ladenburg in his article in the "Forum" of January, 1896, which appeared on the day the bill H. R. 3338 was introduced in the House of Representatives. The following extract will show the nature of his suggestion : —

The next important step is the centralization of our banking system by careful development of our clearing house system, in such a manner that the now disconnected banks of this country shall mutually unite for certain purposes and eventually form a national clearing house bank, which would act for this country somewhat in the same manner as the great central banks of England, France, and Germany.

Briefly, my idea is about as follows : —

Let banks of any kind, in every city or small district, combine in the formation of a kind of clearing house bank, to whose regulation and inspection they would be subject, in addition to state or national laws.

Allow such clearing house banks to perform all the functions now assumed by the clearing houses, and gradually to extend the same by acting as depositaries for bank reserves, etc., opening regular accounts and loaning its funds, but doing business only with its members.

Let the directors of such clearing house banks be elected in such a way that only a few are changed every year, — such election to be determined by the votes of the members according to the average amount of their deposits in the year past, and let the members be responsible for their clearing house bank in the same proportion as their vote for directors.

Let these city or district clearing house banks combine on the same conditions and for the same purpose in a state clearing house bank, and eventually these state clearing house banks could form a national clearing house bank. When this is accomplished we would have a central institution of finance, dealing with its members only, which would represent all the banks of the country, and be guaranteed by them, and to it should be ultimately delegated all power to issue currency. It would be the great central reservoir, from which, indirectly, every little bank in the United States would derive its strength to supply its customers with bank-balance money and currency, and it would by judicious management give confidence and a stability to commerce not hitherto experienced in this country.

I lay great stress on not allowing any of the clearing house banks to do business with any one except its members; but ultimately the national clearing house bank should be given limited power to act as a bank of deposit for the government, and to deal in gold to such an extent as may be necessary to preserve general confidence. Some national legislation may be needed to carry out this idea, but a very substantial and beneficial beginning could be made without it.

Future historians will refer to the last decades of the nineteenth century to show how Americans — so great in many other respects — chased financial rainbows, and unsuccessfully tried all kinds of remedies for fancied and real ills before they intrusted their finances to properly trained men, as they had previously found it expedient to do with their army and navy, their health departments, their courts of justice, their colleges, etc. Finance is not yet accepted as a science by us, probably because our country is so rich that so far it has been able to stand unscientific experiments that would have ruined almost any other nation. The Germans, who have been forced by necessity to husband their resources, have made enormous strides since their finances have been managed by a great central institution — the Reichsbank — under the leadership of the best talent. France and England have long been envied for the comparative stability and safety of their finances, which is due to the workings of their great central banks. We can yet outdo them all, if only we apply the same common sense to our finances that we apply to other departments.

Ours is the richest country in the world. We should be and can be the most powerful nation financially and every other way; but, to accomplish this, we must dispel all doubt as to our financial unit, we must centralize our banking system, and we must manage our finances on scientific principles.

This clear and comprehensive statement of Mr. Ladenburg's views adds to the regret all felt at the loss in their prime of abilities so distinguished. It would be difficult, however, to draw a bill to meet the requirements of this outline, and at the same time avoid the "prejudices arising from the history of the former United States Bank," of which Mr. Ladenburg was well aware. It is natural for those who have received their commercial education in a foreign country to underestimate the acceptance of finance as a science in this, and to overestimate the value of foreign models and banking customs. The science of finance is probably not so well understood in any other country by so large a percentage of the people as it is in the United States.

The difficulty encountered in reconciling foreign ideas with the political principles of our nation shows that our banking system must be formed on the lines of our political faith, and by those who are in sympathy therewith.

SUGGESTION OF PROFESSOR SIDNEY SHERWOOD, OF
JOHNS HOPKINS UNIVERSITY.

In the "Review of Reviews" of January, 1897, among many expert opinions on currency reforms, Professor Sherwood of Johns Hopkins University advocates the incorporation of clearing houses, making them the redemption agencies for the issues of banks. His words are as follows: —

The clearing house associations should be incorporated by federal law. The various sub-treasuries would be mainly government agencies for dealing with the clearing house associations. To the extent to which the sub-treasuries should deposit moneys with the clearing houses the latter should, under proper regulation, be charged with the obligation of redeeming "greenbacks," the government then being relieved, if it chooses, of the necessity of maintaining its gold reserve. Bank notes should no longer be redeemable by the government, but at the respective clearing houses to which the issuing banks belonged, with central redemption at New York. This would make the clearing house in reality a great banking corporation, but it would simplify the whole machinery of banking, and would enable the government to go out of the banking business without conferring unrecompensed privileges upon the banks.

BILL H. R. 171 OF HON. J. H. WALKER, CHAIRMAN OF COMMITTEE ON BANKING AND CURRENCY, FIFTY-FOURTH CONGRESS.

To the earnestness with which the Committee on Banking and Currency of the Fifty-Fourth Congress, from almost the moment of their appointment, solicited interviews, expressions of opinion, suggestions of measures and drafts of bills, for the solution of the financial and banking ills of the country, is in great measure due the preparation of the bill found on page 130.

For the patient and attentive consideration given by the Committee to all who have made suggestions and other communication to them, a most hearty acknowledgment is due, in which it is my pleasure to join.

One cannot examine the volume of the "Hearings and Arguments before the Committee on Banking and Currency of the Fifty-Fourth Congress," without being impressed with the ability and great labor and faithfulness to public duty there manifested.

While I would not have it supposed that there was any special approval of my suggestions by the members of the Committee, it is nevertheless proper to call attention to the second of the "advantages to the banks" proposed to be accomplished by Chairman J. H. Walker's bill H. R. 171, as follows: "Second: A great advantage will be gained in the system of clearing houses provided for in the bill. They will firmly unite all the banks in the country into one system without increasing the financial responsibility of one bank for another. (See Appendix O, p. 60.)" The appendix here referred to is composed of the first three pages of my statement given on page 98 of this volume, which I am gratified to have the chairman adopt and incorporate in his argument. The provisions in Mr. Walker's bill concerning clearing houses are as follows : —

SEC. 17. That the Comptroller may issue to the national clearing house, provided for by section sixty-two, or to any banking association organized under this Act, the greenbacks described in section six to any amount approved of in writing by the Secretary of the Treasury, in addition to the amount issued under section six : Provided, That the association applying for such additional notes shall deposit in the United States Treasury or sub-treasury bonds in kind and amount acceptable to the Secretary of the Treasury, as security for such notes, and shall pay interest on the sum of such notes so issued at such rate as is fixed by law to be paid on loans by the State in which the bank or clearing house is located, such interest on such notes to be paid at such time and in such manner as the Comptroller of the Currency may determine. But a sum no more than ninety per centum of the par value of any bond shall be issued in such greenbacks.

SEC. 18. That any association depositing bonds and receiving greenbacks secured thereby, as provided for by section seventeen, may withdraw such bonds so deposited after thirty days from the date of such deposit upon paying the accumulated interest on the notes issued upon the deposit of such bonds up to the date of their withdrawal, and in addition to such interest shall deposit with the Treasurer lawful money or greenbacks, issued to associations under section six of this Act, or mixed, to an amount equal to the greenbacks issued to the associations under section seventeen and for which the bonds were deposited for security ; but no more than five per centum of the greenbacks issued to any other one association under section six of this Act shall be accepted as a deposit for the withdrawal of such bonds.

SEC. 19. That the notes deposited for the withdrawal of bonds shall be immediately put in redemption and the money received for them shall be kept as a special fund with which to redeem and destroy the amount of greenbacks issued to the association under section seventeen of this Act, and such greenbacks shall be destroyed equal in amount to the greenbacks issued to the association when the bonds hereinbefore mentioned were deposited to secure such notes.

SEC. 57. That any five or more national banking associations are hereby authorized to unite in forming a clearing house association. By adopting a constitution and by-laws the banking associations certifying the Comptroller of the Currency that fact shall in that act become a clearing house association body corporate, upon such constitution and by-laws being approved in writing by the Comptroller of the Currency.

SEC. 58. That any changes in the constitution or by-laws of any such association, to become valid, must be approved in writing by the Comptroller of the Currency, and the Comptroller may annul any part of the same at any time after a hearing thereon, with the concurrence of a majority of all the board of advisers.

SEC. 59. That clearing house associations shall be subject to like examination by national bank examiners as national banking associations, and shall make such reports as the Comptroller of the Currency may request.

SEC. 60. That any incorporated banking association may be admitted to membership in any clearing house association incorporated under this Act; and the membership of any banking association may be terminated by any action of the clearing house association approved by the Comptroller of the Currency.

SEC. 61. That each member of such clearing house association shall share in its fees and other income, and in its assessments, expenses, and losses in the proportion that the sum of its capital, surplus, and undivided profits bear to the sum of all the capital, surplus, and undivided profits of all the associations composing the clearing house association as shown by the annual report of the Comptroller of the Currency last made previous to the apportionment of the same.

SEC. 62. That five or more clearing house associations organized under this Act may form a national clearing house association upon the same terms and conditions as those governing in the case of clearing house associations composed of banking associations : Provided, however, That national clearing house associations may buy and sell such bonds as are necessary to the conduct of their legitimate business to any amount and of any kind approved of by the Comptroller of the Currency, and may provide for the coin redemption of currency notes of banking associations, and may take and issue, under the provisions of section seventeen of this Act, the greenbacks described in section six, in denominations of not less than one thousand dollars.

SEC. 63. That any clearing house association organized under this act may be designated by the Secretary of the Treasury as a depository of public money and may also be employed as financial agent of the government.

SEC. 64. That each clearing house association may make loans to or borrow from other clearing house associations, and banking associations may make loans to or borrow from clearing house associations. In all such loaning and borrowing clearing house and banking associations shall be exempt from the usury laws of the States in which they are located.

SEC. 65. That any clearing house association organized under this Act may establish a department for the clearing of currency notes of banking associations in the current redemption of such notes.

SEC. 66. That any clearing house association organized under this Act may deliver to the Treasurer of the United States or to any assistant treasurer of the United States, for safekeeping, any kind of money or bonds, and receive such a statement of the fact of their being in the Treasury of the United States as the Secretary of the Treasury may approve.

Sec. 67. That any banking association may withdraw from any clearing house association, and any clearing house association may withdraw from the national clearing house association upon such conditions as the Comptroller of the Currency may approve.

These sections propose to accomplish the great desideratum of the incorporation of clearing houses under government supervision. An emergency currency is provided under sections 17, 18, and 19, but the security is to be "bonds in kind and amount acceptable to the Secretary of the Treasury." Such a currency would provide a market for the bonds used, but it would be no benefit to the commerce of the country. Wheat, cotton, and corn could not in any form be accepted. The business community has no interest in a currency so created or in the incorporation of clearing houses for the object of obtaining an emergency currency in this way.

National banks have under the present law the privilege of taking out currency on pledge of bonds up to the amount of their capital stock, as provided in section 17. But they do not avail themselves of it. In the panic of 1873 the privilege was unused to the extent of $345,000,000, and in 1893 to $427,000,000. These figures prove that the privilege of taking out currency on government bonds is of no great benefit to commercial banks. If section 17 allowed bank assets to be pledged with the clearing house as trustee, by its bank members, and all clearing houses were required to accept such notes at par, the provision would be of real benefit to the business community. But in its present form section 17 confers no privilege additional to those enjoyed under the present law.

The functions of clearing houses described in sections 62–66, inclusive, are of doubtful value, and in many particulars trench upon the business transacted now by banks. Banks should be strictly graded, that is, all business that can be transacted by the popular banks should be reserved for them. The higher grade of banks should only perform those acts which the lower grade is not competent to do.

It is further to be noticed that the clearing houses are not divided into districts by States, and many other important provisions are omitted in these sections. It is, however, a great advance in the discussion that the incorporation of clearing houses under a federal law should be thus proposed and ably discussed as it afterwards was by the Committee and the Comptroller of the Currency, Mr. Eckels.

Mr. Walker considers it a recommendation to his bill that "it firmly unites all the banks in the country into one system without increasing the financial responsibility of one bank for another." I would ask, Why should not the great clearing houses of the country be willing, even be required, to be responsible for each other to the extent of accepting at par the notes issued by each? The banks of issue of Germany are compelled to receive at par each other's circulating notes; that was a provision of the Indiana state banking law, and the same principle underlaid the old state bank systems with their branches. If the state clearing houses of issue hold approved collateral security for all their currency obligations, as trustees, why should it be considered a great request to ask the banks to accept themselves the currency which in the first place they offer to the public, when thereby the great boon of stability and freedom from panic will be secured to the commerce of the nation?

It is to be noted, however, that this firm union among the banks is placed among the advantages they will enjoy from a graded system, and none will acknowlege the truth of that statement more readily than bank officials who were burdened with the responsibility of management during the panic of 1893.

### HON. MARRIOTT BROSIUS,

member of the Committee on Banking and Currency, House of Representatives, Fifty-Fourth Congress, made the following statement before the Committee : —

I am unalterably opposed to the federal government conferring upon any body of men under a free banking law the power to issue circulating notes on their own property under their own control.

If a bank currency is to be issued to conform to this opinion, the security therefor must be placed with a trustee, who shall act as between the note-holder and the bank. Mr. Brosius here states a fundamental proposition, and in no way can it more easily be carried into effect than by incorporating clearing houses and authorizing them to act as such trustees.

### HON. WILLIAM L. TRENHOLM,

Comptroller of the Currency under President Cleveland's first administration, is the most recent advocate of the incorporation of clearing houses under a federal law. His suggestions to the Monetary Commission (November, 1897) are as follows : —

First. To make adequate provision for the recognition of existing clearing houses and the establishment of others by allowing them to be organized in central reserve cities under the national banking law, with defined powers and responsibilities.

Second. To empower clearing houses thus organized to license banks in their respective cities to accept circulating drafts drawn by banks in places where there are no clearing houses, such drafts to be free of all taxation, federal, state, or municipal, and to be payable to bearer.

## PLAN OF HON. W. L. TRENHOLM 229

Third. To limit the maximum amount to which any such bank may have acceptances outstanding at any one time to a certain proportion of its capital and surplus.

Fourth. To prescribe that no such bank be licensed to accept such drafts without taking from the drawers adequate security therefor to the full amount of such contemplated acceptances, which security may be in the form of discounted paper; also, without having deposited with the clearing house security to the amount of the circulating drafts applied for, the sufficiency of such security, both in amount and character, to be certified in each instance separately to the Comptroller of the Currency by the proper authorities of the clearing house and approved by the local bank examiner. Securities so deposited to be released only upon presentation to the clearing house of canceled drafts, which drafts are to be delivered by the clearing house to the Comptroller of the Currency for destruction.

Fifth. The circulating drafts authorized to be accepted under the above conditions may be drawn by any national bank, or by any state or private bank which will submit to such examinations by the local examiner as may be prescribed by the Comptroller of the Currency. The amount of drafts of any such drawer outstanding at one time to be limited to a proportion of its quick assets, including those held by the accepting bank.

Sixth. The circulating drafts so authorized shall be of uniform design, and may be in denominations of $1, $2, $3, $5, and multiples of $5, having engraved upon their face the name of the accepting bank, with blanks to be filled with the names of the drawers.

Seventh. Such circulating drafts to be prepared by the Comptroller of the Currency and issued to each clearing house association upon its requisition, made from time to time under regulations to be established by the Comptroller of the Currency.

Eighth. This plan, if adopted, is expected to work in the following manner: A clearing house association will from time to time make requisition upon the Comptroller of the Currency for a certain amount of such circulating drafts to be accepted by certain named banks, members of that association. The banks for whose benefit such circulating drafts are called for will satisfy the authorities of the clearing house association as to their compliance respectively with the requirements of the system; whereupon issues will be made to such banks, and each of such banks will cause to be filled in the name of the drawer and then execute its acceptance upon the face of the drafts. These drafts may be then sent as incomplete currency is now sent through the mails or by express at a moderate charge, as they will not become effective from circulation until duly signed by the drawers. When signed they will be paid out by the drawing bank or banker for local use first, and will gradually find their way back to the accepting banks, where they will be redeemed and sent into the clearing house, in order to release a proportionate amount of the securities there held against such issue. The object of this suggestion is to enable banks at remote points throughout the country to meet the local demand for currency when it arises, and only as it does arise, and at the same time to limit and control such issues through the operation of the principle of self-protection, which will assert itself in the management of the accepting banks.

## CONCLUSION.

These various opinions, while they indicate that the development of the clearing house has been widely considered, show also the need of gathering together the arguments and facts supporting the idea, so that they may not evaporate and be lost as factors in the discussion which must continue until the question is settled.

It will be noticed that the suggestions in the minds of the different writers all came from experience of the satisfactory working of clearing house certificates. Should not that be legalized which has been well done extra legally, and should not all the country receive the benefits which have thus far been experienced by only a part?

# INDEX

ACCOMMODATION, an enlarged, a remedy for lost confidence, 114.
Accumulations, dangers from, 173.
Ambler, D. G., suggestions of, for financial reform, 217.
American and English finances, instability of, 8.
American institutions produced a general banking law, 101, 104.
Apprehension minimum, the, of Walter Bagehot, 18.
avoided by a trusteed currency, 70.
in the United States, 38, 39.
Asset-security defined, 90.
Assets, the commercial, of banks form the strength of clearing house currency, 117.
paper money, issued against those of banks, 166.
Associations of banks required, 129.
Atkinson, Edward, xvi.
plan of secured notes, 213.

Bagehot, Walter, theory of apprehension minimum of, 17.
Baltimore plan, the, almost unanimously abandoned, 93.
a restrictive one, 111.
described, 119.
Bank assets in the hands of the banker or a trustee give elasticity, 90.
Bank currency, history of, in the United States, 178.
Bank of England, formation of, 2.
abuse of powers by, 4.
fairness of dealings of, 14.
leads English banks, 16.
no power beyond its cash reserves, 16.
takes first step in panics, 17.
protects reserves by restriction, 18.
a standing menace, 19.
taken in tow by bank of France, 20.
not a good model, 20.
competitive, 21.
referred to, 29, 42, 43, 68, 69, 102, 103, 107, 181, 200, 202.
suspension of charter of, 15.
Bank of France. See France, bank of.

Bank of Germany. See Germany, bank of.
Bank failures, one third preventible, 86.
Bank functions, separation of, 2, 3, 4, 5.
Bank, governmental, disapproved in the United States, 102.
Bank, the United States, overthrown by Jackson, 115.
Bankers have but an indirect interest in the purchase of silver by government, 106.
position of, regarding a new system, 93.
Banking act, the national, affords insufficient protection, 153.
Banking capital of the country all pledged for a clearing house currency, 118.
Banking ends in clearing house, 99.
Banking functions, separation of, 1.
Banking, a graded system of, abolishes competition, 29.
a graded system compared with a competitive, 48.
Banking ideas, progress of, 181.
Banking, the operation of, 99.
share of clearing houses in, 101.
Banking system, the American, can it be made more stable ? 8.
the national, a glory of republican institutions, 95.
national, completion of, 152.
when broken down, 10.
Banking system, defects in, lead to panics, 109.
Banking systems, graded and ungraded, 6.
two classes of, 186.
Banking, three kinds of, 178.
Bank notes universally receivable in Germany, 35.
Webster on, 1.
Banks cannot unite on a plan for a new system, 93.
in different sections classified, 72.
in the East and West compared, 57.
force liquidations, 111.

graded system of, does away with competition, 29.
of high grade demanded, 45.
individual, do not form a true system, 99.
inspection of, 100.
of issue few under the German system, 88.
joint action of, through clearing houses, 103.
multiplication of, does not change principle of competition, 68.
should serve borrowers, 47.
the specially chartered, 180.
suffer but slightly from enforced liquidation, 112.
suspended, outcome of, 85.
Baring guarantee fund, the, 20
Baring panic, the, of 1890, 16.
Barter, a strictly cash basis, 10.
Bill intended to provide solid credit, 114.
Bill to protect credit, features of, xiv., 130-151.
Bonds, government, not a good basis for currency, 123.
not held largely by commercial banks, 205.
Bond-secured currency of little value, 92, 226.
Bond-security defined, 90.
Bonds as security for paper money, 163.
Borrowers should be served by banks, xiv., 47.
Branch banks, ix., 187.
a foreign suggestion, ix.
Fauchier's opinion of, 27.
State banks with branches, 187.
un-American, 95.
"Bryan States" and "McKinley States," 72, 73.
all comparisons favorable to, 78.
Brosius, Hon. Marriott, chairman of sub-committee in Congress, 98.
remarks by, 228.
Boston Boot and Shoe Club, 213.
Bullion Committee, the, of 1810, 176.
Bullion Report, the, of 1810, made to Parliament, 19, 114, 201, 205.
Business of the country the basis of clearing house certificates, 169.

Capital, the banking of the country pledged in a clearing house currency, 118, 119.
idle, abhorrent to the business man, 161.
remunerative employment of, 10.
Cash reserves of a bank not large, 107.
inadequate, 17.
Cash valuations universal, 80.
Certificates, clearing house, 196, 230.
issue of, xiv., 42.
type of an elastic currency, 89.

Chartered banks, characteristics of, 191.
Charters, special, granted in some States, 186.
Checks, the universal use of, 205.
Circulation, profit on, 128.
Clapier, M., opinion of the financial system of France, 2.
Clearing house as trustee, 71.
the New York, features of certificates of, 168.
suspends when the stock exchange suspends, 64.
Clearing house certificates, 196, 230.
issue of, 42.
why issued, 205.
Clearing house currency, features of, 126.
plan of Charles Parsons for, 209.
retired when not needed, 173.
sources of the strength of, 117, 118.
very little would be issued, 96.
Clearing house system, plan for extending, 197.
Clearing houses, bill to incorporate, xv., 130.
can be made a high grade of bank, 45.
delicate functions of, 100.
enjoy the confidence of the community, 124.
incorporation of, under federal law, xiv., 70.
incorporation of, the capstone on the American system, 104.
must be brought under federal law, 45.
of issue, remarks on, 116.
must be organized, 100.
Clearings fifty thousand millions annually, 99.
Cobb, Hon. Seth W., member of congressional committee on banking, 98.
Circulation, an unsecured, in 1837, 83.
Coin, the immense reserve of, in France, 30.
balances only paid in, 9.
in the Bank of France, 24.
paper, to old expression, vi., 12.
permanence of, as money, 159.
Collection, public not interested in modes of, 89.
Collections, cash, of suspended banks, 88.
Commerce, Chamber of, in Paris, 7.
Commerce, lessons from history of, 11.
lifeblood of, flows into the bank tills, 111.
Commercial credit, support of in Germany, 36.
Commercial honor, in England, 14.
Commodities exchanged must be the basis of paper money, 167.

## INDEX

Competition, absence of, in the French banking system, 28.
between banks impossible in Germany, 36.
between English banks, 29.
in the United States system, as in the English, 38.
principle of, not changed by multiplication of banks, 68.
should be abandoned, 47, 48.
system of, dangerous, 83.
Comptroller of the Currency winks at infraction of law, 43.
Conant, Charles A., on the German system, 32.
Confidence the basis of the value of paper money, 162.
impossible under present conditions, 61, 62.
in a secured currency, 204.
remedy for failure of, 177.
Congress, the country must look to for its national banking system, 104.
in control of banks and currency in 1863, 184.
must be the source of a better system, 94, 95.
must pass necessary laws, 8.
should make clearing houses a part of the national banking system, 155.
should not permit banks to issue currency and hold the security, 202.
Continental finances, stability of, 7, 8.
Contraction produces a dangerous stringency, 66, 67.
and expansion explained, 90.
Convertibility an essential of good currency, 45.
of the German bank notes, 36.
Coöperation, not competition, peace, not strife, the law of banking, 70.
Copper syndicate, collapse of, in France, 26.
Corruption resulting from state bank legislation, 182.
Cotton, currency secured by, safe, 82.
Cotton, wheat, and cattle, command gold in New York and Liverpool, 80, 81.
Country banks, reserves of, 52.
weak spot in reserves of, 53.
Credit, all business conducted on, 108.
loss of, without infringement of law, business mistakes or error of judgment, 153, 154.
commercial, bill to protect, 98.
necessity of upholding it by legal measures, 11.
protected by the Imperial Bank of Germany, 36.
Credit currency authorized, 20.
Credit Lyonnais, the, compared with the Bank of England, 69.
Credit, Webster on, 108.

Credit system, the, demands stability, 9, 10, 13.
origin of, 107.
the, should be made to work smoothly, 110.
the universal, 10.
an unprotected, answerable for panics, 107.
Creditors own the cash in banks, 175.
Creed, the financial, of the United States, first article in, 101.
second article in, 121.
third article in, 124.
Crop, the annual, of insolvent notes, 120.
Currency, a, between banks, 196.
two types of, 89, 90.
the two classes of, 160.
Commission, the, of the United States, 180.
the bond-secured, inelastic, 89, 90.
clearing house, should be limited, 172.
clearing house, elements of strength of, 169.
common-law right to issue, 183.
common-law right to issue withdrawn, 179.
important dates in history of, 5.
disappears in a day in time of panic, 112.
elasticity of, if secured, 89.
for emergency, 205.
an emergency, to be guarded, 88.
government, not discussed, 11.
the, of government not issued in accordance with the national banking act, 106.
issue of, forbidden in four States, 185.
a national, benefits of, 164.
must be convertible into coin, 125.
must be taken by banks at par, 45.
to be at par everywhere, the third article of the financial creed, 124.
principle, the, vs. the reserve principle, 29.
regulation of, 1.
regulation of, Lord Overstone on, 199.
a safety valve, 205.
secured and unsecured, 192.
a secured, a panacea, 200, 206.
a secured, the second of the accepted financial doctrines of the United States, 121, 122.
that is secured commands confidence, 204.
security of, under special charters, 193.
a trusteed, relief from, 70.
unsecured, contracts with fearful velocity, 203.

Dates, two important, 5.
Dead line, the financial, 54, 61.

## 234   INDEX

Debtors, should they take care of themselves ? 110.
Debts, foreign, paid by the West and South, 80.
Demand payment indispensable, 89.
Departmental banks and local currency proposed in France, 27.
Deposit reserves valueless in an emergency, 59, 60.
Deposits and reserves in the United States, 40.
Depositors bound to a bank by favors, 203.
Difficulties discussed, 72.
Directors in banks control issue of currency in England until 1844, 2.
Discount, rates of, in France, 25.
Discount, raising the rate of, 19.
Discounting conservative under supervision, 87.
Distrust prevents assistance, 62.
no test of solvency, 69.
Drummond, Henry, on security, 199.
Dunbar, Professor C. F., on the German financial system, 31, 32.
on the credit of German bank notes, 35.

East and West, banks in, compared, 57.
Elastic currency, defined, 90, 92.
Elasticity obtainable with a secured currency, 89.
Emergency currency, an, 205.
Charles Parsons's plan for, 209.
England and France, systems of banks compared, 28.
England, banking system of, 14–21.
a standing menace to commercial peace, 19.
where it fails, 14.
England, formation of the Bank of, 2.
the source of common law, 181.
panics in, 15, 20, 16.
theory of reserves in, 17.
England, Bank of, a central power, 102.
lacks an essential requisite, 29.
the model in America at first, 181.
relief from suspension of charter of, 15.
Equilibrium, Peel's law of, 201.
Examples from foreign lands, 6, 7.
Exchange, the New York Stock, assistance from, 63.
Exchanges effected by paper currency, 167.
Expansion and contraction explained, 90, 109.
Expansive method for relief in panics, 113, 114.
Expansive nature of a clearing house currency, 172.
Experience, bitter, in 1893–1897, 8.

Failures, in 1893, 84.

Failures of banks, one third preventable, 86.
caused by sudden demand for liquidation, 60.
Fallacious remedies, 65.
Farm products, comparison of loans with, 77.
ten times the bank discounts, 82.
Faucher, Léon, on departmental banks, 27.
Fellowship among banks, examples of, 129.
principle of, 121.
principle of, in the guarantee by all clearing houses, 171.
Fiat notes, a form of fixed currency, 165.
Finances of government not discussed, 12.
distinct from those of commercial banks, 106.
Fixed currency, definition of, 160.
sound, 162.
Forced liquidations, relief from, 16.
France, bank of, 7, 16, 22, 115.
a central power lacking in the United States, 102.
effects of its large reserve, 26.
effects of the war of 1870 on the Bank of, 25, 26.
enormous power of, 26.
established, 22.
not a monopoly, 23.
privileges and regulations of, 23.
restores prosperity, 47.
solidity of, 24.
strengthens all the banks in France, 28, 29.
France, banks of, not competitive, 28.
Chamber of Deputies of, establishes the Bank of France, 22.
financial system of, 21.
grades in, 29, 36.
indemnity to Germany, 1870, 26.
in 1847, 97.
panics not known in, 28.
simplicity of its banking system, 25.
France and England, bank systems of compared, 28, 29.
France and Germany, stability of banking systems of, 11.
France and Germany, systems of, compared, 34.
Free banking, principle of, established, 183.
Free banking law of New York, 2.
Functions of banks, separation of, 1, 5.

Gallatin, Albert, on banks in his day, 182.
General banking law does not contemplate banks of great capital, 101.
the first article of the financial creed, 101.

# INDEX 235

General banking laws found only in the United States, 101.
states having, 187.
universal in 1863, 184.
in accordance with republican institutions, 184, 189.
and special charters compared, 188, 190.
development of banking under, 189.
General publicity demanded under general banking laws, 191, 192.
German banking system borrows from Peel's act, 32.
Germany, financial system of, 31.
grades in, 33, 36.
Germany, Imperial Bank of, protects credit, 33, 36.
power to increase its issue *ad libitum*, 32.
Germany, legal reserve of, 34.
system of, 88.
and France, banking systems compared, 37.
stability of banking systems of, 11.
systems of compared, 34.
Gilman, Theodore, statement of before congressional committee, 98.
Girard, Stephen, bank of, 182.
Gold, run for, produced by panic, 113.
Government bonds not a satisfactory basis for currency, 123.
finances not discussed, v., 11.
notes a form of fixed currency, 165.
when wisely issued, 12.
Gradation, system of, ix.
Grades of clearing houses of issue, 116.
of French banks, 29, 36.
of German banks, 33, 36.
Greenbacks, retirement of, no remedy, 68.
Growth, area for greatest, in the West and South, 73.
Guarantee of the banks associated, an assurance of safety, 71.

Hill, Hon. Ebenezer J., member of congressional committee on banking, 98.
Hoarding currency to be avoided, 127.
done away with by the proposed law, 156.

Imperial Bank of Germany, the, 32.
privileges of, 88.
Independence, Declaration of, principles of, 6, 104, 181.
second declaration of, 184.
Indiana, laws of to insure security, 194, 196.
Inflation does not affect relation between reserves and liabilities, 65.
a hollow mockery, 66.
Insolvent notes, annual crop of, 12.0
Interest, rates of, irregular in the United States, 39.

Iowa, laws of to insure security, 194, 196.
Issue, indefinite, theory of, 33.
Issue, banks of, in Germany, only those of highest grade, 35.
Issue and discount, separation of, 200.
Issue, power of, liable to abuse, 201.

Jackson, President, on the United States Bank, 115, 182.
his victory, 188.
Joplin, Thomas, on protection of the public, 199.

Kentucky, laws of, in regard to security, 194, 196.

Ladenburg, Adolph, xvi.
article by in the Forum, 218.
Lavergne, M. Léonce de, opinion of the Bank of France, 23.
Law to incorporate clearing houses features of, 46.
Legislation needed to cure and prevent evils, 44.
Liquidation, apprehension of, 39.
Liquidations, forced, defined, 110.
relief from, 16.
severe on distant communities, 79.
Liquidation, the late, has ruined business, and relief is demanded, 47.
Liverpool, Lord, opinion of, 14.
quoted, 179.
on a secure currency, 198.
Loan and trust companies have small reserves, 40.
Loans by a clearing house committee to tottering banks might be made with safety, 87.
Loans and discounts, comparison of, 77.
offer a fallacious protection in panic, 62.
Lombard Street, Walter Bagehot's book on, 18.
London, immense wealth of, 21.
Loss and delay to be guaranteed against, 125.
Loyd, Samuel Jones, influences the English banking laws, 2, 3.

MacLeod, on the expansive method of dealing with panics, 114.
on the fantastic theory of equilibrium, 201.
on restriction of credit, 113.
opinion on the action of the Bank of England in a crisis, 20, 103.
" Theory of Credit," 19, 30, 178.
McCulloch, J. R., on a secured currency, 170.
Manufactured products, comparison of loans with, 77.
Marcy, governor, on paper money, 180.
Metal and paper currency, 159.

Metals, the precious, qualities of, 160.
Monarchical examples antagonized, 6.
Monetary Commission of 1888, the, 7.
of 1897, 228.
Money, a common denominator, 80, 81.
Money, paper, Charles Moran on, 157.
Money question, the, what it is, 110.
Money, Republican or Democratic, 94.
supply of, diminished by contraction, 67.
Monopolies, Secretary of the Treasury on, 183.
Moran, Charles, on security for paper money, 157.
Mortgages, comparison of loans with, 78.

Nation, one bank thought sufficient for, 181.
National banking act, the, 42, 184.
National banks, reserves of, 50.
Nevada desires to relegate control of banks to the national government, 185.
New York, bank of the State of, report by, in 1837, 179.
financial law, 1838, 122.
free banking law of, 2.
law of 1838, 198.
New York and Ohio systems examples of general laws, 190.
North, the, adopted general laws, 190.
Note circulation of the Bank of France, 24.
Note-holder, the, at a disadvantage, 123.
needs a trustee because he cannot investigate the banks, 123.
Note-holders have no feeling for the banks, 203.
necessarily act for themselves, 203.
Notes, insolvent, should be paid before the liquidation of the bank, 126.
mutually exchangeable in Germany, 32.
to be issued, limited under special charters, 192.

Ogden, J. de P., on banks of issue, 199.
on the importance of the New York banking law, 184.
Over-issues, people of the United States opposed to, 12.
Overstone, Lord, on banking, 199.

Panama Canal, collapse of, 26.
Panic, definition of a, 21.
the, of 1837, 1.
the, of 1837, origin of, 200.
losses by, estimated at six thousand millions, 109.
the "Baring" (1890), 16.
of 1890, in England, united action of banks, 103.

of 1893, a test period, 152.
of 1893, incident in, 63.
might have been stayed by slight assistance, 86.
inaugurated by forced liquidations, 16.
Panics, the, of 1884, 1893, and 1895, 108.
are they begun by banks? 42.
arise in England and the United States, 30.
begin in England and the United States, 7.
bill to prevent, 114.
can only be prepared for by arrangements made on general principles, 84.
causes of, 93.
come like squalls, without notice, 84.
do not arise in Germany, 34.
do not occur in France, 28.
freedom from, demanded, 10.
immunity from, guaranteed by a clearing house currency, 126, 127.
importance of preventing, 176.
losses by, 109.
money loss from, incalculable, 112.
nature of, 107.
protection from, 174.
ravages of, 11.
result from a loss of credit, 115.
safeguards against, 105.
stopped by forced liquidations, 111.
two methods of dealing with, 109.
why do they rise in the United States? 13.
warded off in Germany by the Imperial Bank, 35.
Paper currency requires safeguards, 166.
Paper money, Charles Moran on, 157.
Paper money, to coin, 12.
Paris, Chamber of Commerce of, 7.
Parsimony, the law of, 161.
Parsons, Charles, statement of, 209.
Passing the ring, game of, 69.
Peel, bill of, founded upon the currency principle, 30.
charter of the Bank of England enacted, 2.
law of equilibrium of, 201.
Peel's act characterized by Professor Dunbar, 31.
Peril from the condition of the banks, 64.
Political principles, fundamental, 6.
Politics in banking, 94.
Price, Professor Bonamy, on a means of controlling a crisis, 19.
Property, comparison of loans with, 77.
Prussia, mutual exchange of bills, 32.
Public, the general, the reservoir of currency, 111.

Receivership, threat of, disastrous, 61.
Redeemable currency defined, 160, 165.
Redemption agencies, fallacious remedies, 69.
Redemption of currency by clearing houses, 88.
Re-discounting a safe use of money, 97.
Reichsbank, the, of Germany, elasticity of, 31.
Republican banking system, how it can be made preëminent, 70.
Reserve of the Bank of France, 24.
Reserve, good effects of the large, in the Bank of France, 26.
of the Imperial Bank of Germany, 34.
what is a safe? 41.
an immense, provided by incorporating clearing houses, 46.
a, obtained without cost, 46.
should be established and secured by law, 154.
Reserves above legal requirements, 53.
average cash, of commercial banks, 40.
condition of, in the United States, 49.
of national banks, 50.
of in cities, 55.
of country banks, 55.
decline of, produces solicitude, 39, 40.
in deposits, 50.
in lawful money, 50.
must not be costly, 45.
offer a common standard, 51.
percentage of, to demand obligations, 52.
protection of, a guarantee of safety, 71.
question of, 10.
how restricted in the United States, 38.
small loss of, produces panic, 43.
smallness of, 54, 58.
surplus, percentages of, 56.
theory of, in England, 17.
Restriction and expansion, 109.
and extra legal measures, 10.
Robinson, F. J., opinion of, 14.
Rothschilds, the, opinion of French solidity, 8.
Runs on banks, 203.
creditors trained for, 175.

Safety, elements of, 71.
Safety valve, none now existing, 127.
a, provided by currency, 205.
Sampson, Mr., of the London "Times," opinion of, 110.
Savings banks, danger to, 158.

Scotland, mutual exchange of bills, 32.
Secured currency, advantages of, 192, 206.
described, 122.
either rigid or elastic, 92.
principle of, from England, 200.
Securities, convertible and inconvertible, 63.
Security, collateral, with a trustee, the demand of the business community, 122.
Security, how attained, 45, 193, 196.
two kinds of, 90.
Sherman, Hoyt, address to Iowa bankers, 121.
on the Iowa system, 195.
on the principle of fellowship, 121.
Sherwood, Professor Sidney, suggestions by, in "Review of Reviews," 221.
Silver scare, the, precipitates a panic, 108.
Smith, Adam, on the first failure of the credit system, 107.
"Wealth of Nations," 170.
South, the, adopted special charters, 180.
South and West, the, suffer most from a bad system, 79.
Southern States, large percentage of lawful money in, 72.
Special charters and general laws compared, 188.
Special charters monarchical in character, 189.
Specie payments the third article of the financial creed, 124.
Stability of the earth no more needful than financial stability, 128.
Stability obtained by incorporating clearing houses, 46.
two conditions of, 9.
the first requisite, 9.
demanded in all parts of the land, xii., 158.
State banks, origin of, 181, 182.
with branches, ix., 187.
State system, the, has its source in democratic legislation, 95.
State systems in the United States, mutual exchange of bills, 32.
States, the, of the Union, classified, 72.
boundaries of, should be recognized in establishing clearing houses of issue, 116, 117.
Suffolk banking system, the, 193.
Sumner, Professor, on the Bullion Report, 114.
opinion of, on bank notes, 115.
test of, met by clearing house currency, 119.
Supervision, the capstone of the American system, 104.
by clearing houses salutary, 87.
Suspended banks, outcome of, 85.

Suspension of bank facilities from loss of reserves, 58, 60.
Surplus reserves, small, 54.
Switzerland, mutual exchange of bills, 32.

Table I. Reserves of national banks, 51.
Table II. Surplus reserves, 54.
Table III. Percentages of surplus reserves, 56.
Table IV. Comparative reserves, 57.
Table V. Deposit reserves, 59.
Table VI. Financial statistics of all States, 74, 75.
Table VII. Percentage of assets to obligations, 76.
Table VIII. Banking situation in seven Southern States, 82.
Table IX. Suspended national banks of 1893, 86.
Table X. Cash collections of suspended banks, 88.
Tariff, the Wilson, produced distress, 68.
Tariff, a sufficient, the panacea for governmental financial troubles, 106.
Test period of the American banking system, 152.
Torrens, Col., on a mistake of the Parliament, 202.
responsible for a change in English banking laws, 2.
Trade, laws of, regulate the amount of currency, 161.
Trenholm, Hon. W. L., suggestions to the Monetary Commission, 228.
Trustee currency, 122.
Trustee, services of a, required by the note-holder, 122, 123.
Trusteeship favors elasticity, 90.

United States Bank, the, 115, 181.
overthrow of, 182.
revival of, desired by some, 95.
United States bondholders do not need aid, 92.
United States law at present inadequate to sustain the credit system, 10, 11.
United States, financial system of, 38.
has all the defects of the English, 38.
how to be made preëminent, 70.
Unions of banks would strengthen national life, 129.

Venezuela message precipitates a panic, 108.
Virginia and Maryland examples of the special charter system, 190.

Walker, Hon. J. H., xvi.
provisions of a bill of, 223.
Washington, remark of, on influence, 202.
Wealth, accumulated, difference in, 72.
Webster, Daniel, on currency, vi., 1.
on credit, 108.
on functions of banks, 199.
on banks and borrowers, xii.
in favor of paper universally convertible, 97.
views about regulation of currency, 2, 4.
West and East, banks in, compared, 57.
West and South, the, suffer most from a bad system, 78.
Western States, large percentage of lawful money in, 72.
Wilson tariff, distress produced by, 68.

www.ingramcontent.com/pod-product-compliance
Lightning Source LLC
Chambersburg PA
CBHW021403230426
43666CB00006B/617